Script Supervising
and
Film Continuity

Second Edition

Script supervisor Pat Miller prompts Director Leo McCarey as he acts out a scene for Cary Grant and Kathleen Nesbitt. (Taken on the set of "An Affair to Remember," a Twentieth Century Fox release. © 1957, Twentieth Century Fox Film Corporation and Jerry Wald Productions, Inc.)

Script Supervising and Film Continuity

Second Edition

Pat P. Miller

Focal Press

Boston London

Focal Press is an imprint of Butterworth Publishers.

Illustrations by Joseph Musso. Additional illustrations by
Mike Dirham and Patrice Marak.

Library of Congress Cataloging-in-Publication Data
Miller, Pat P.
    Script supervising and film continuity/Pat P.
  Miller.—2nd ed.
      p.   cm.
    ISBN 0-240-80018-4
      1. Cinematography. 2. Motion pictures—
  Production and direction. 3. Continuity. I. Title.
  TR850.M54 1990
  791.43'0233—dc20   89-23373

British Library Cataloguing in Publication Data
Miller, Pat P.
    Script supervising and film continuity. —2nd ed.
    1. Cinema films. Continuity
    I. Title
    791.43'0233

    ISBN 0-240-80018-4

Butterworth-Heinemann
313 Washington Street
Newton, MA 02158-1626

10 9 8 7 6 5 4 3

Printed in the United States of America

This book is dedicated to the often unheralded continuity (née script) supervisors, whose craft is an integral part of filmmaking.

Contents

10   Techniques of Coverage   163

11   Techniques of Matching   183

Foreword

Pat Miller's book on script supervision is the first, and insofar as I am aware, the only complete and thorough work of its kind ever published. It covers in detail the hundreds—and I mean literally hundreds—of tasks a good script supervisor must perform: the recording of how the director is shooting the scene; if a master, how he breaks it up; a description of each shot, including who is in it, etc.; where there are changes in the dialogue or action that would affect the story line; how the characters are dressed; how the characters are positioned, and in what direction they are looking; the points at which the characters sit, stand, or otherwise move; the times at which characters enter and exit, and whether or not their actions accord with the scenes that precede and follow; whether or not the action matches from one cut to the next; how long the scene runs in screen time; which lens was used; whether the camera was stationary or moving and, if the latter, when movement occurred; whether the take was good or not, and why; and so on, ad infinitum.

No one but an experienced person in the field could possibly have written such a full treatment of the subject, since it reveals not only the various problems confronting the supervisor but also the most efficient methods of handling them. Most important, though, is the fact that the text is written in language that is simple, unaffected, and understandable.

I consider the book a genuine breakthrough for those who aspire to become script supervisors, and in my opinion it can be read with profit by many others in our business: beginning directors, assistants, editors, and, in fact, those in every branch of our industry.

The importance of a good script supervisor is a fact of which I have always been conscious. He or she is a must for a smooth and successful production, but I never realized the amount of work necessary before and after shooting that the script supervisor had to do.

I recommend the book heartily. It is sorely needed, and a job well done.

Vincent Sherman

Preface

This book touches on many aspects of filmmaking. But its primary purpose is to serve as a definitive guide book for one of the industry's highly essential yet insufficiently acknowledged crafts: script supervising and film continuity.

The movie industry generally uses the title Script Supervisor for the person on the set who is responsible for maintaining the continuity of the film. The name, unfortunately, is a misnomer and therefore causes misconceptions about what a script supervisor actually does. Actually, the script supervisor has nothing to do with creating, altering, or supervising the script per se. Rather, the script supervisor is concerned with the images that the director extracts from the script and transmits onto film. In essence, the script supervisor is the liaison between the director and the film editor throughout the complex procedure in which a script is converted to a motion picture. And what is widely acknowledged by those in the industry is that script supervising and film continuity constitute a vital phase of the filmmaking process.

In Hollywood's "old days," when women usually performed this job, the even less appropriate title of Script Girl was awarded. Yet when I apprenticed at the major studios, as early as 1952, I was taught by two male script supervisors, and the president of the Script Supervisors Guild—now Local 871 of the International Alliance of Theatrical and Stage Employees (IATSE)—was a man. So the term *script girl* is a glaring anachronism, even though it is still found in film-industry publications. Here's an excerpt from

Guide to Filmmaking by Edward Pincus (reprinted by arrangement with the New American Library, Inc., New York, NY, copyright © 1969, 1972, page 66).

> . . . details and continuity of action must match from shot to shot to allow for continuity editing. In Hollywood filming there is a script girl whose special function it is to make sure that such disconcerting changes do not occur within a scene.

So even as late as 1972, and beyond, the title Script Girl lingered.

In a book titled *Magic of Film Editing*, by Joseph F. Robertson (Tab Books, Inc., Blue Ridge Summit, PA, 1983), the author bestows a compelling commentary on the craft—and uses the masculine pronoun to refer to the script supervisor.

> The script supervisor is the director's right hand . . . the link of communication between the editor and the director. . . . [He] is objective and highly intelligent. . . . Without the script supervisor, the director can be destroyed. . . . The script supervisor communicates directly with the editor by means of script notes. This is a precise form of communication worked out through many years of effort on the part of the director, the script supervisor and the editor. . . . Notes will be the bible for the film editor. . . . A producer or director would be very wise to make sure he hires a top script supervisor. A bad one can add weeks of film editing time. . . . If the film editor has to do all the research himself, it can cost the production an untold amount of extra money, time and grief.

Another tribute to the script supervisor appeared in the April 1984 issue of the *American Film Magazine,* published by the American Film Institute. Tom McDonough, the author of the article "Tender Is the Light," wrote: "script supervisors are solemn standup comics whose shtick is solid geometry."

When men joined the ranks of script girls the title was changed, first to Script Clerk (a demeaning label), then to Script Supervisor, which still gives no indication of the complex nature and major responsibility of the job. My aim is to officially change that title and put a whole new slant on the meaning of this unique craft. And it is to be hoped that this book will finally lay to rest the title Script Girl. A more substantive title to use in a screen credit is Continuity Supervisor.

In years past, when most films were produced exclusively by major studios, there were intensive apprenticeship programs for the various crafts people who comprise a motion picture crew. But in the present era of independent production companies, film technicians must learn their skills by taking educational courses or by having a professional friend or relative train them in a specific craft. Training is now catch-as-catch-can, whether acquired in classrooms removed from the real action or on the often frenetic set itself, and usually without proper prior instruction.

There is nothing better, of course, than on-the-job experience. Yet everyone has to begin somewhere. So this book provides a practical introduction to this unique profession—a prelude to apprenticeship. There are no books before this one that delineate the methodology of script supervising and film continuity. By studying the how-to's copiously depicted in this volume and acquiring the basic tools in advance, you will have enough usable knowledge to proceed to active involvement on a studio sound stage and thus pursue a fulfilling career in the fascinating business of filmmaking.

Furthermore, this book provides a comprehensive overview of the combined technical and aesthetic elements that go into the making of a motion picture. So it should also be of interest to those who are curious about, or aspiring toward, other film work, such as script writing, film editing, and film directing.

The novice *script writer,* in becoming familiar with the metamorphosis that takes place when a script is transferred to the screen, will glean how to properly structure a screenplay or a teleplay and thereby enhance its sale potential. A producer will be more interested in a good story that has already been developed into a viable script, because it will save the expense of extensive rewriting by a professional script writer.

The fledgling *film editor* will gain a comprehensive overview of what transpires on the set as the script is transformed into numerous pieces of film that an editor assembles into a well-crafted motion picture. The book contains vital data related to film editing and includes a sample of the final continuity script—the editor's blueprint for cutting. Much can be learned before setting foot inside a studio editing room.

The fledgling *film director* will gain awareness of some of the camera's idiosyncracies with regard to filming, and thus will be in a position to avoid technical pitfalls when rehearsing the dramatics of a scene.

It is virtually impossible to enumerate all the technical and philosophical challenges that a continuity supervisor encounters in the course of filming a show. But the basic fundamentals depicted in this book will stand you in good stead because they explore the nuts and bolts of making a motion picture or television show. And the text is replete with industry terminology, so you will readily assimilate film language.

In preparing the second edition of this book, I endeavored to cover the impact of the more current technology in film and television production—particularly on the function of the continuity supervisor with the advent of tape and video systems. What I have learned is that the innovations do not affect the existing work patterns of the conventional continuity supervisor. The new technology relates mainly to the mechanical aspects of camera and film-editing apparatus. So for the time being—although video technology may send us off on another tangent—filming as we know it today is not an endangered species. It's safe to state that after learning a few techniques and indigenous terms and clerical details, the film continuity supervisor can easily switch to tape and video production. But, conversely, someone proficient only in tape and video production would be hard-pressed to handle the craft of continuity supervising in feature films and films for television.

Because a goodly number of women have in recent years entered the production crafts whose workers have heretofore been given masculine labels (e.g., *cameraman, boom man, sound man*), I've made the effort to avoid using a gender designation in any of the job titles.

Acknowledgments

I wish to express special thanks to the following people for their help and encouragement: Iris Chekenian, Lily La Cava, Gene Fowler, Marjorie Fowler, Joseph F. Robertson, Sinara Stull, Meta Wilde, Gloria Morgan, Anne G. Schlosser, Peggy Jago, Donna Montrezza, and Jae Carmichael. And I wish to express my gratitude to Robert Gary and Grant Loucks for graciously answering my questions in preparing the second edition; also, a special thanks to the editorial staff at Focal Press.

1

Getting into
the Act

VISIT A STUDIO LOT AND
SOUND STAGE

If you have never visited a movie studio while filming is in progress, try to do
so as soon as possible. If you have no friend or relative to get you in, cultivate
a new acquaintance! A sure way to get in is to apply for any kind of a job in a
studio.

A studio lot is a complex of sound stages and buildings housing the
equipment, offices, and personnel connected with the production of feature
pictures or television shows. In industry parlance, the process of transmit-
ting a live performance onto film is referred to as "shooting the scene."

For someone who has never been on a studio lot, here's a warning: *Heed
the red light.*

Sound stages are marked with huge numbers on their outside walls.
There is also a red light above every door or on a stanchion just outside the
doors. When that red light is blinking, it means the filming of a scene is in
progress. *Do not open the door* to peek in or to enter the stage. Why? Because
the squeak or slam of the door will be picked up on the sound track, causing
an actor's speech to be obliterated, or if the scene is lit for darkness or other
special effects, a shaft of light from the outside may well ruin what is being
photographed. In each instance, the scene might have to be done over. You
have possibly shattered a delicate mood and, worse, caused an annoying,
time-consuming, and costly disturbance. So I repeat: *Heed the red light.*

1

Another word of caution: Never carry any kind of a camera onto a sound stage. You will be summarily asked to leave the premises, and there is the possibility that your camera will be confiscated.

Inside the Sound Stage

Now that you have entered the inner sanctum of the sound stage, try to remain there for the better part of a day. Carefully observe all the activities. Much may be incomprehensible at first, but before long you will be able to identify the various technicians at work. You will find one individual, however, whose work will be difficult to fathom. That is the *continuity supervisor.*

You will observe that the continuity supervisor is making notes in a letter-size book (known as the *script*) and conferring with the director, the actors, the director of photography, and other studio personnel. Essentially, the continuity supervisor is recording information that the editor needs to know: how the director is transforming the script into motion picture scenes that audiences will see on the screen in theaters or on television sets.

The continuity supervisor is also involved in other phases of film production that are not as visible. These phases are depicted in succeeding chapters.

QUALIFICATIONS FOR THE JOB

Continuity supervising is a multifaceted and highly responsible job. In order to become eligible, there are mandated prerequisites and requisites.

Prerequisites*

- □ An analytical mind and a keen sense of organization.
- □ A sharp eye for visual details and a good ear for sounds.
- □ Composure under stress and the ability to function with aplomb when the atmosphere is fraught with tension and speed is required.
- □ A high level of energy to sustain you during the long days and nights of a shooting schedule.
- □ Ingenuity to improvise whenever circumstances arise that were not covered during your training or encountered in past experience.

---

* If you do not possess the necessary prerequisites or are unable or unwilling to acquire them, then you would be wise to pursue another vocation.

- ☐ A pleasing personality, well-mannered deportment, and good grooming.
- ☐ Typing skills and some form of shorthand or speed writing.
- ☐ Legible handwriting or hand printing.
- ☐ An aptitude for basic arithmetic.
- ☐ A respectable command of the English language.

Requisites*

- ☐ Expertise in reading a script to analyze and break it down according to standard procedure for filming scenes *out of continuity.*
- ☐ Knowledge of screenplay and teleplay forms. It is suggested that you read as many scripts as possible because many script-writing innovations have been introduced in recent years, and you have to be familiar with their structure. There may be times when part or all of a scene will be performed *ad lib,* that is, not according to the written dialogue and description in the script. In that case, you will have to record the improvised scene or scenes in the particular form of script at hand. (Here is where your speed writing and typing skills are a great asset.) Even more challenging is the case when a scene goes into rehearsal, and sometimes even into filming, *without* benefit of a script. In that event, you are the only person who has a record of what has been put on film.
- ☐ An understanding of the dynamics of camera direction and progression. Both subjects require skill in matching camera angles and action cuts.
- ☐ Knowledge of the techniques for rehearsing and cuing actors.
- ☐ The ability to time performances and calculate picture-running time.

TOOLS OF THE TRADE

Script binder (pinch-back or three-ring)
Stopwatch
Typewriter
Pencils (lead and colored)
Pencil sharpener (mechanical pencils eliminate sharpener)
Scratch pads
Ruled yellow foolscap pads
Carbon paper
Typing paper
Paper clips
Stapler and staples
Staple remover
Three-hole punch
Hole reinforcements

---

* If you will methodically study the instructions detailed in the ensuing chapters, you will acquire the knowledge and skills that will prepare you for a career in continuity supervising.

Ball-point pens	Envelopes (legal size)
Erasers	Manila folders (with clasps)
Ruler (attached to script binder)	Index tabs
Scissors	Dictionary
Transparent tape	Flashlight
Correction fluid	Timepiece*
Brads	Camp stool**
Rubber bands	

FILM CONTINUITY IS A CRAFT

And what is continuity? Curiously, the principle of continuity is the keystone of motion-picture production.

In a legitimate stage performance, the story is enacted in a chronological manner. That is, the curtain rises on Act 1, which is followed by Act 2, Act 3, and the final curtain. This formula is not carried out when a film is constructed. (Films for television are crafted in much the same way as major feature pictures, only the pace of operation is accelerated.)

Like the scripts for stage plays, scripts for motion pictures and television shows are written in chronological order. But the similarity ends there. In motion picture and television productions, the actors do not perform the scenes in the sequence shown in the script. Instead, the scenes are shot *out of continuity*. In other words, all sequences that take place in a given locale—no matter when they occur in the time frame of the story—are scheduled to be performed and filmed during one time period. This modus operandi was devised for economic reasons. It is very costly to equip (*rig*) a sound stage for filming. Extensive preliminary measures are involved in fabricating a movie stage set; these include constructing overhead scaffolds on which a network of lights is mounted, building a structural framework according to the production designer's specifications, and installing whatever equipment is required to make the set suitable. It would be cost-prohibitive indeed to move from set to set in following the story's realistic sequence.

---

* An accurate wristwatch or pocket watch is an essential tool because it is your official duty to record the time of the first shot of the day, the time lunch was called, the time of the first shot after lunch, and the time the last shot of the day was finished. This daily report goes to the production office on a special form, which will be described later.

** For your own comfort, you might carry a small camp stool to squeeze into tight camera spots or take to outdoor locations when chairs are not available.

As a consequence of the eccentric way in which motion pictures are constructed, the film editor receives an assortment of disjointed pieces of film that must be assembled and structured into cohesive, smooth-flowing dramatic episodes, as though the scenes had been performed and filmed in customary storytelling sequence. Because it is not feasible for the film editor to be in attendance during the shooting, a comprehensive record of all that takes place on the sound stage or location where shooting is done is needed. And inasmuch as the continuity supervisor functions as the liaison between the director and the editor, it was a natural consequence that the continuity script became a guidebook for the editor—a blueprint, as it were, of how all the pieces fit together. Included are notations of deviations from the original script and important notes on the director's preferences concerning the final cutting and editing of the picture. Thus, the continuity script has evolved into the editor's "bible." An example of a continuity script in final form is shown in Chapter 7.

SHOOTING OUT OF CONTINUITY

To further explain the concept of shooting out of continuity, let us assume that three scenes in a script take place in the kitchen. The supposition, therefore, is that for as long as it takes to commit all three sequences to film, the efforts of the actors and the crew will be concentrated in the kitchen set.

But there is another twist in the scheme of filming scenes out of continuity. The shooting schedule lists Scene 37, Scene 46, and Scene 2 to be shot in that order (for reasons best known to the production planners). Consequently, the actors will perform their roles in that convoluted sequence.

In the chronology of the story, Scene 37—the first scene to go in front of the camera—takes place twenty-five years after Scene 2. For this scene, the actors are made up to appear twenty-five years older and are dressed in contemporary clothes. The décor and accoutrements in the kitchen are also contemporary.

The next scene to be shot is Scene 46, which takes place only a few days or weeks after Scene 37. The set, décor, and the actors' makeup remain much the same, with the exception that the actors are in different wardrobe. Sometimes only a change of wardrobe lets the audience know that there has been a passage of time (today's movie and television audiences are very sophisticated).

Finally, Scene 2 is scheduled for filming. Now all the furnishings in the room are changed to transform it into an old-fashioned kitchen of the era; the actors are made up to appear twenty-five years younger than they looked in Scene 37 and are dressed in the fashion of the period.

WHAT THE CONTINUITY
SUPERVISOR OVERSEES

There are several concomitant elements in the process of filming scenes out of continuity that mandate the continuity supervisor to keep a watchful eye.

1. Let us picture the three kitchen scenes that have been filmed. In each segment, we saw the actors come in (*enter*) through the kitchen door (from, say, the back door). They spoke their lines (*dialogue*) and sat at the table or moved into positions prompted by the director. We saw them walk out (*exit*) through another door (into, say, the dining room). According to the production schedule, the dining-room and backyard sequences are scheduled to be filmed at some future date. When those connecting scenes are enacted before the camera, the actors must appear exactly, in every minute detail, as they were when they entered and exited the filmed scenes.

Each department has its responsibility to ensure editing continuity: the wardrobe department makes sure that the actors are dressed correctly; the makeup department makes sure the actors' makeup is correct; the hair-dressing department makes sure the actors' coiffures are correct; the property department makes sure all the hand props carried by the actors are correct.

But the continuity supervisor is concerned with myriad infinitesimal details in each of the related scenes: the top button of an actor's shirt was open as he entered Scene 2, and he was wearing a sweater as he exited the room; an actor's hat brim was rolled on the right side as he entered Scene 37, and his coat collar was turned up on the right side as he exited the room; the left corner of a shirt collar was outside the jacket as the actor entered Scene 46, and he exited the room without the jacket; a cigarette, smoked one-third down, was in the actor's left hand as he exited Scene 37; an actor was wearing eyeglasses as he entered Scene 46 and he put them in his jacket pocket when he exited; an actress's nail polish was pink in Scene 2 and dark red in Scene 37; an actress was wearing three rings in Scene 2 and two rings in Scene 46 (description of the rings and on which fingers they are worn is also important); a belt was tied in a bow to the right side of an actress's dress in Scene 37; an actress was wearing pearl button earrings in Scene 46 and gold hoops in Scene 2; the actress pushed her hair behind her right ear as she crossed to the window before she exited Scene 2; an actress entered Scene 46 with a purse in her left hand; an actress exited Scene 37 with the strap of her purse over her left shoulder.

Every one of the above details must be carefully matched for the actors' appearances in the scenes that precede and follow the kitchen scenes.

2. In addition to meticulously matching makeup, props, and wardrobe, the continuity supervisor must be cognizant of other details: At what pace did the actors enter and exit the kitchen? Did they dash or saunter through the doorways? (The entrances into and the exits from the connecting sets must be made at exactly the same pace.) Who followed whom?

Were the doors open or closed at the start of each sequence, and how were they at the finish?

3. In each of the three kitchen segments, the actors gave a continuous performance of dialogue and movement (much the same as in a stage play). That is known as *shooting a master scene*. Now another filmic convention comes into play.

After the master shot has been completed, the next undertaking is *covering* or *breaking up* the master. The terms mean the same and are used interchangeably. Covering (or coverage) is defined as the shooting of different camera viewpoints and closer angles on the same action and dialogue as that played in the master shot. These component angles may feature three, two, or just one of the group of characters in the scene.

Every *cover shot* necessitates the repetition of either all or a portion of the master scene's dialogue and movements. The camera is focused on the individual character or characters while the other actors deliver their lines from *off-camera* (OC). This phase of filming calls for special skill on the part of the continuity supervisor. Each actor whose turn is *on-camera* has to be gently reminded of what his or her movements were during the performance of the master, and this must be done with utmost delicacy and diplomacy.

On what word was a puff of a cigarette taken with the left hand? On what word of another's speech was a cup picked up with the right hand (with or without the saucer)? On what word was a fork with a bit of potato on it lifted in the left hand? On what word did the little girl turn to speak to the person on her left while her braid fell to her right shoulder? On what word did the strap of the actress's gown slip off her left shoulder? On what word did an actor stand up or sit down? On what word were legs or arms crossed right-over-left or vice versa? On what word was the right hand placed on the hip, and when was it taken down? On what word did an off-camera actor stand up or sit down (this would change eye contact, requiring others to look up or down)? At what point in the dialogue did another actor enter or exit the scene? The list of possible matching actions is limitless.

The filming of the requisite cover shots in each of the three kitchen sequences may take days, weeks, or longer, depending on the complexity of the scenes.

The techniques for scene matching and action matching are delineated in Chapters 9, 10, and 11. In the practice of these techniques, the craft of the continuity supervisor becomes highly visible.

ONLY ONE CONTINUITY SUPERVISOR

You are now ready to be ushered into the challenging and fascinating world of script supervising and film continuity. But first I must inform you of an important qualification.

Most departments of a film company consist of a key person plus a few assistants who handle details, but there is only *one* continuity supervisor for every show. Yours is a completely autonomous position. Should illness or death or gross incompetence cause your absence while filming is in progress, there is no one in the company to take over for you; a substitute continuity supervisor has to be called in. This predicament may incur a delay in filming and, consequently, additional expense for the production company. And what a Herculean task it is for the script supervisor who has to take over at a moment's notice without the essential prior preparation.

So before you contemplate this engrossing career, be sure you are in robust health and can endure working long and laborious hours. Movie-making is as arduous as it is glamorous.

2

Dealing with
the Script

FIRST COMES THE WORD

The written material from which a motion picture or television film is crafted is called the *script*. The material undergoes many modifications before it is considered a *shooting script*. A script written for a feature film is termed a *screenplay;* a script written for television is termed a *teleplay*. The script's fundamental format is the same in either medium: each master scene is numbered sequentially, followed by auxiliary numbers that denote various camera angles within the master scene. Following is a sample first act of a teleplay.* In this sample, Scene 3 is the number of the master shot; it indicates the locale where the action takes place. The consecutive numbers that follow (4, 5, 6) are the auxiliary numbers that suggest different camera angles. Consequently, Scene numbers 3 through 6 constitute the master scene. Script writers, however, often devise variations on the basic format. So I urge that you read as many scripts as you can lay your hands on and familiarize yourself with writers' innovations.

---

* Episode of "The Brian Keith Show," written by Perry Grant and Dick Bensfield.

```
                              ACT ONE


            FADE IN:


      1.    EXT. SEAN'S FRONT DOOR - NIGHT

            It is late and dark.  SEAN comes up with a suitcase and
            a flight bag.  He is tired.  He unlocks the door and
            enters.  He is wearing a Hawaiian shirt and slacks.


      2.    INT. SEAN'S LIVING ROOM - NIGHT

            The lights are out.  Sean enters.  He yawns.  He is tired
            and wants to go right to bed.  He sets down his bag, then,
            as he heads toward the bedroom, he takes off shirt and
            casually tosses it onto a chair or sofa.  He enters the
            bedroom.


      3.    INT. SEAN'S BEDROOM - NIGHT

            The lights are out.  Sean enters, kicks off his shoes
            and slides out of his pants.  Down to his shorts, he
            sighs, yawns, then slides into bed, stretching out.
            After a beat, a female arm comes lovingly across his
            chest and a sweet, female voice says...
                              CELIA'S VOICE (O.S.)
                        I love you.


      4.    WIDER ANGLE

            Sean's head snaps toward the voice.  He finds himself
            nose to nose with a lovely young bride, CELIA.  She
            gasps.  Sean reacts.
                                 SEAN
                        What the...!

                                 CELIA
                              (screams)
                        Ahhh...!

            She grabs the blankets up around her.


      5.    ANOTHER ANGLE

            DAVE, the groom, bursts in from the bathroom.  He wears
            a bathrobe.  Light comes in from the bathroom.

                                              (CONTINUED)
```

Figure 2.1

2.

5 (Cont.)

                    DAVE
          Baby, what is it?

6.   ANGLE ON SEAN

     He is halfway out of bed, still not certain what this is all
     about. He whips his head around to look towards the new voice.
     It has all happened in a split second. We FREEZE FRAME,
     catching him in an awkward position, halfway out of bed.

                                        CUT TO:

7.   INT. SEAN'S LIVING ROOM - NIGHT

     Sean, Celia and Dave are there in robes. MOE is there in
     uniform. Dave is holding his arm protectively around Celia.

                    MOE
          You wanna press charges, Doc?

                    DAVE
          What do you mean? He attacked
          my wife.

                    MOE
               (to Sean)
          Sorry, Doc...it's my duty to
          inform you of your rights.

                    SEAN
          I didn't attack her. I just got
          in bed with her.

8.   ANGLE ON FRONT DOOR

     MRS. GRUBER lets herself in. Celia comes up to her.

                    CELIA
          Mrs. Gruber, thank goodness. Will
          you tell them you rented it to us?
          They don't believe us.

                    GRUBER
               (sees Sean)
          What are you doing here?

                    SEAN
          I live here.

                                        (CONTINUED)

8 (Cont.)

                GRUBER
You weren't supposed to be
back for a week.

                SEAN
Well, I'm back now and I got
mugged in my own bed.

                MOE
              (to Dave)
You have the right to remain
silent. You have the right to
seek counsel.

                DAVE
Officer, she rented this place
to us.

                SEAN
              (to Gruber)
You rented my apartment without
my permission?

                MOE
              (to Gruber)
You have the right to remain
silent...

                SEAN
Moe, will you shut up.

                GRUBER
Dr. Jamison, if you'd just once
listen to reason. It is my property
and this young couple is on their
honeymoon.

                CELIA
And our reservations fell through.

                DAVE
I told you. The hotels are packed.

                GRUBER
I found them sitting on a bench...
on their wedding night. You said
you'd be away, so, being a romantic
person, I let them stay here.

                SEAN
For a modest fee, no doubt.

                      (CONTINUED)

4.

8 (Cont. 1)

                    GRUBER
          Just a breakage deposit.
                (trying to explain this)
          Well, I was just thinking about
          the night of my third wedding.
          Mario was a gymnast.

                    CELIA
                (tearfully)
          What are we going to do?

                    DAVE
          I guess we'll have to leave.

                    SEAN
                (relenting)
          Well...no. You can't leave in
          the middle of the night. I'll
          sleep on the sofa. You kids can
          have the bedroom.

There is silence as bride and groom exchange glances.
They obviously don't want Sean so close by.

                    SEAN
                (getting the message)
          Okay, I'll find someplace.

                    GRUBER
                (quickly)
          There's no room at my place.

                    SEAN
          I wouldn't trust you, anyway.

                    MOE
          Doesn't anybody want to be informed
          of their rights?

                              DISSOLVE:

9.   INT. RECEPTION ROOM - DAY

      PUNI adjusts some flowers in a vase, picks up the vase and
      starts with it towards Sean's office. DR. CHAFFEE enters.

                    CHAFFEE
          Good morning.

                    PUNI
          Morning, Dr. Chaffee.

                              (CONTINUED)

5.

9 (Cont.)

> CHAFFEE
> Puni, I've told you and told you...
> stop putting flowers around.

> PUNI
> But Doctor, this is Hawaii.

> CHAFFEE
> I don't care. They're full of
> pollen. They'll make my patients
> sneeze.

He exits into the corridor. Puni looks after him and
makes a face.

> PUNI
> Yankee, go home.

CUT TO:

10.   INT. SEAN'S OFFICE - DAY

Puni enters and sets the vase of flowers on his desk.

11.   ANOTHER ANGLE

Sean, wearing a rumpled sport shirt and pants, is stirring
on the sofa where he apparently has spent the night.

> PUNI
> Dr. Jamison, what are you doing
> here?

> SEAN
> (stretches, feels back)
> I've been asking myself that all
> night.
> (rubs back again)
> Ohhh...
> (gets up)

> PUNI
> But, Doctor, why couldn't you
> sleep in your own bed?

> SEAN
> It was two against one...

Puni reacts.

CUT TO:

HOW TO READ A SCRIPT

From the preceding sample teleplay, you will discern that a typical page of script consists of three major elements: the locale or set, the business or action, and the dialogue.

1. The Locale or Set

This is the site where the master scene (the *Establishing Shot*) takes place. The locale is always written in capital letters and designates whether the scene takes place indoors (INT.—interior) or outdoors (EXT.—exterior). The time element is always indicated; e.g., 1. INT. KITCHEN—DAY, or 2. EXT. RESIDENTIAL STREET—NIGHT. The designation of DAY or NIGHT in the master-scene heading quickly conveys to the director of photography (cinematographer) and the gaffer (key electrician) the basic lighting for the set. If a day scene takes place indoors, sunlight will come through the windows; if it is a night scene, darkness will be seen through the windows, lamps will be lit, and perhaps lights will flicker from a background piece of scenery.

Sometimes a scene marked EXT. is not actually filmed outdoors. Instead, the exterior scene is built inside the sound stage. Studio craftspeople are capable of duplicating an exterior set so realistically that the audience cannot detect that the filming was done indoors rather than outdoors. When the story calls for rain or other atmospheric conditions, the artistry of the *special effects* department reproduces the inclement weather. In that way, the scenes are filmed under controlled conditions—a more convenient arrangement than subjecting cast and crew to the whims of Mother Nature.

Nowadays, however, shooting is done in all natural environments and under natural weather conditions. The rain and snow fall where they may, and the actors and technicians get soaked and chilled. (If you know you are going to be so subjected, always carry some aspirin or other cold remedies on your person.)

When an exterior scene is to be filmed outdoors, the master scene heading will include the word LOCATION. The actual address will be listed in the first assistant's *Shooting Schedule*. The word LOCATION may also appear for an interior set when that scene is to be filmed at a place other than the sound stage. Shooting anywhere away from the sound stage is designated LOCATION.

When (STOCK) is written alongside the locale, it means that the scene will not be filmed by the company crew but will be procured from a film library (the term *archive* is sometimes used). During the editing process, that piece of extraneous film will be cut into the final picture. Stock shots are always indicated in the script; e.g., EXT. LOS ANGELES AIRPORT—ESTABLISHING SHOT—DAY (STOCK), or 4. EXT. DOWNTOWN BUSINESS DISTRICT—NIGHT (STOCK).

2. The Business or Action

The written description of what takes place in the scene is referred to as the *business* or the *action*. The text describes the general movements of the characters, their physical appearance and distinguishing marks, and the essential details of the décor and ambience of the set. Everything written in the script, except the dialogue, is referred to as business or action.

3. The Dialogue

All the words spoken by the actors are called *dialogue* (or referred to as speeches). The dialogue is written in a narrow column down the center of the page. Each speech is headed by the character's name in capital letters.

The words in parentheses under the character's name indicate the *mood* or *motivation*. These designations are the author's concept of the emotions that the actors should display. Sometimes the mood or motivation is suggested in the business or action part of the script. Example:

Albert gazes *ruefully* at his burned-out house.

ALBERT
Everything's gone! Everything.

When dialogue is to be spoken in unison, that is, two voices speaking simultaneously, the speeches are written side by side:

JOHN	MARY
(startled)	(startled)
What are you doing here?	What are you doing here?

If AD LIB is written in the script, you should be on the alert when shooting that scene. The script may read, "The two couples meet in front of the church, AD LIB greetings." This is fine for the written script: the reader then visualizes the scene. But in filming the script, every spoken word is picked up by the stage microphone (*boom*) and recorded. Therefore, your continuity script to the editor has to include the actual words spoken in the ad-lib greeting. Your revised page might read as follows:

MARY AND JOHN (IN UNISON)
Well, hello, there.

AGNES
Mary, it's good to see you.

JOHN
How ya doin', Tom?

When (OS) or (OC) is written alongside a character's name, it means the voice is coming from *off-screen* or *off-camera*. This could be from another part of the room or another location. The speaker is not on film at this particular spot in the scene. However, the speaker may or may not be put on film subsequently, depending on the director's discretion. At times in the final editing, only the VOICE is heard as it plays for a reaction on the face of an on-camera actor.

Sometimes the letters OS may denote any sound that comes from off-screen or off-camera.

When (VOICE OVER) is written *in place of* a character's name, it refers to the voice of a speaker whom the audience will not see—frequently a voice heard over a public address system at an airport or train station, a voice coming from a radio or television set, or the voice of a narrator heard over the photographed scenes. At the time of shooting that portion of a scene, the "voices" are usually delivered by the director, the first assistant director, an actor pressed into service, or the continuity supervisor. Later, in final editing, these voices are replaced with recordings of professional voices.

HOW TO BREAK DOWN A SCRIPT

First and foremost, read the script. Read it, read it, and read it again. Become thoroughly familiar with the story line and the characters.

Primarily, *breaking down* the script consists of marking each page with notations that will enable you to spot salient details at a glance during pressured shooting hours. A helpful hint: use different colored pencils to underscore different elements in the script, and be consistent throughout. That way, you can quickly spot the pertinent information you need on the page. When shooting is in progress, speed and accuracy are high priorities.

The following numbered paragraphs formulate a practicable routine for breaking down a script. While the record-keeping models depicted in this book have proven very efficient (after years of trial and error), they are mainly for guidance. You may devise any system that is easy for yourself, so long as the records are thorough and accurate and all the information is readily accessible, and so long as your method enables you to reply quickly and accurately to the numerous and urgent questions that will be tossed at you.

1. Master Scenes

Underline each numbered master scene—always identified in capital letters. The master scene constitutes a single segment of the scenario wherein a continuous performance is staged in a specific setting (locale). Every new locale signifies another master scene.

As noted on page 9, the numbers written in conjunction with the master scene denote camera angles. These represent the author's designations regarding continuity. However, the director's cinematic concept may differ substantially. As continuity supervisor, you will revise the script, when necessary, so that those numbered scenes reflect the director's concept—for that is what will be seen on the screen.

At times, some extraneous scenes will be interjected into the master scene, such as POINT OF VIEW (POV), FLASHBACK, or MONTAGE. These scenes should be underscored as master scenes, because they will be staged and filmed separately from the original master. The term CUT BACK means returning to the action of the original scene following the interruption of any extraneous scenes.

The *point of view* shot refers to what is seen from the actor's point of view as he observes something off-camera (OC) or off-screen (OS). It may be an object or a scene of activity. In the confines of a stage play, the actors verbalize what they see off-stage, and the audience visualizes it. But in the dramatics of filmmaking, when actors look off-camera and react, the audience's curiosity has to be satisfied by showing the activity or the object that the actors are observing.

The *flashback* is a storytelling technique by which past events or images are interspersed (intercut) with contemporary scenes. Some flashback scenes call for special cinematic effects, which are done in a film laboratory.

The term *montage* is used for a series of quick shots that depict a passage of time, a sequence of events, or different images that sharpen a story point or intensify the suspense of a scene.

The interjected scenes, as written in the script, are of course viewed in proper sequence within the master scene. But that is accomplished in the editing room. The editor artfully intercuts these extraneous but relevant scenes into a comprehensive sequence.

Writers do not always designate individual scene numbers for POV, FLASHBACK, or MONTAGE. Often the descriptions of these interrelated scenes are included in the business/action part of the script or expressed in dialogue. Example:

23. INT. SERGEANT MARTIN'S OFFICE-DAY

In a darkened room, a group of people are viewing slides projected on a screen. Martin's VOICE explains each picture.

                    MARTIN
          That's our suspect posing as a gas
          attendant.

A CLICK, and another slide appears.

                    MARTIN
          That's our man playing tennis at the
          Wilshire Country Club.

CLICK, and another slide is flashed on the screen.

MARTIN
There he is betting on the horses at
Santa Anita.

The pictures in those slides are in the category of montage. In all probability, and in adherence to filmic convention, those pictures will be transformed into action scenes and filmed for the benefit of the audience. (More on this under "Slating Extraneous Scenes" in Chapter 6).

According to traditional screenplay or teleplay format, the end of a scene or sequence is designated by a term such as CUT TO, DISSOLVE, WIPE TO, or FADE OUT. But contemporary writers have taken the liberty of dispensing with these end-of-scene designations. So the only way you know that a scene or sequence has ended is to recognize the following scene as being a master scene. The unmistakable clue is the notation of a different locale in capital letters.

Draw a line across the page to separate each master sequence.

2. Story Chronology/Time Breakdown

Mark each sequence with the chronological *time lapses* that manifest the progress of the story, e.g., 1st Day (indicated as D-1); 2nd Day (D-2), sometimes written as NEXT DAY; 3rd Night (N-3) which may take place three weeks, or three years, later in the story and should be so noted; 4th Night (N-4); 5th Day (D-5), which may take place two months later, and should be so noted. Mark the correct chronological number of the time lapses at the right-hand margin alongside each captioned master scene. When a sequence takes place later the same day or night, I place a plus sign (+) alongside the number, rather than spell out "later that day" or "later that night." If a master scene runs for more than one page, make the notation at the upper right-hand corner of each page of that master scene. This makes for speedy reference and eliminates the time-consuming flipping of pages in order to find information needed instantly (see pages 27–31). Prepare a Story Chronology/Time Breakdown (see page 32).

3. Time Elements/Day or Night

Underline the particular time of A.M. or P.M. when indicated. The scene caption may include: DAWN, MORNING, LATE AFTERNOON, DUSK, MOONLIGHT, etc. Once again, this information refers to the basic lighting of the set and is a guide for the director of photography and the gaffer (they mark their scripts accordingly). Sometimes a special time factor crops up in the business portion (i.e., reference to a time on a clock), or mentioned in dialogue ("I'll meet you after school"). Watch out for such clues and make notation alongside the scene caption; also, make notation of this pertinent time factor on the pages of any scenes that precede or follow (see point 9). Your conspicuous notation will alert you to be concerned about the wardrobe, makeup, or props. Time lapses crucially affect these elements. Here's another lighting situation that's gleaned from dialogue. For example:

Mary enters the living room.

MARY
Jim, why are you sitting in the dark?

During the performance, blinds will be opened to let daylight in, or a light will be switched on, or perhaps a candle will be lit, if the script is for a period story. You should make notation at the caption of the scene that the room starts in *darkness* and goes to *lights on;* also, alert the gaffer of the light change.

By the same token, if a scene starts with an illuminated room and the lights are switched off during the performance, you should make the notation "Light Change" at the caption of the scene and then mark the page at the point where the room goes to darkness.

4. Names of Characters

Underline the names of the characters as they are revealed in each scene. The first time a name appears in the script, it is written in capital letters. Subsequent references to this name are then written in upper and lower case; underscoring is not necessary.

5. Characters' Physical Distinctions

Underline the written descriptions of the characters. But keep in mind that the physical characteristics described by the author may not always correspond with the features of the actors or actresses cast for the parts. The script may mention a buxom blonde, but the actress cast for the role is a slinky brunette; or the script may call for a handsome, macho young man, whereas the actor cast for the part is corpulent and bald-headed.

As soon as possible, ask the director or the first assistant director if the actors cast for the roles fit the descriptions in the script. If not, you will have to alert the actors of the necessary departures from the script before they memorize dialogue containing erroneous descriptions. For instance, John, speaking to Harry, says, "Did you get a look at that buxom blonde in the accounting office?" Instead, it should be "that slinky brunette." These changes are critical when shooting out of continuity, so be on guard when specific images are mentioned in dialogue, and alert the actors whose speeches are affected (revised pages do not always get to the actors in time).

6. Overt Action

Underline the *overt action* written in the business and mood descriptions in the script. Overt action means the conspicuous things that the characters do in a scene, e.g., engage in a fight, hug, kiss, pace the floor, read a book, feed the baby, parachute out of a plane, break props, smoke feverishly, ring a doorbell, put on or take off garments, or any such physical action.

The underscored overt action on the page will instantly apprise you of the overall business in the scene. This is very helpful when shooting is done rapidly and under pressure.

It is also good practice to underscore when characters *enter* and *exit* the scene. By using one color to underscore entrances and another for exits, you can instantly spot the comings and goings of the characters within the scene.

These signals are helpful when breaking up a master scene that runs for several pages.

7. Props

Underline references to props or make note of them in the margins. There are two kinds of props:

a. *Hand props* are articles that are handled by the actors, such as pipes, eyeglasses, suitcases, crutches, newspapers, briefcases, books, or any such articles.

b. *Stage props* are articles that are placed as significant dressing in the set, such as candlesticks on a table, a vase of flowers on a piano, pictures on a desk or mantelpiece, desk plaques, clothing placed on furniture, or any such visible item.

Among stage props are *breakaway props*. These are articles of set dressing that are used in overt actions, such as a vase that is broken over someone's head, a wooden or glass door that is shattered, or a chair that falls apart when sat upon. Special sound effects that simulate the breaking of these props are put in later, during the editing.

Once again, props are often mentioned in dialogue—watch out for those speeches and make the necessary notations.

8. Read the Script Again

In rereading the script, you will frequently discover some vital detail in either the dialogue or the business that escaped your attention in previous readings. The detail might be an essential *carry-over* from one scene to another, relating to props, makeup, wardrobe, chronology, the weather, or whatever. Just one small word may trigger the need to add notations to preceding and subsequent scenes that are affected by the carry-over detail.

9. Back-Matching Notes

When details carry over from one scene to another, you must make accurate notes on the affected pages. This is called *back matching,* and introduces the dogma of *direct* and *indirect* continuity.

Direct continuity occurs when a condition or a detail (some business or prop) carries over from one scene to the next consecutive scene with no time lapse. For example, in Scene 1 (EXT.) a man uses a key to open the door of his house from the outside. There is a newspaper under his left arm. The shot ends (*is cut*) as the man puts the key in the lock with his right hand. In Scene 2 (INT.) the man enters the house. But it may be days and even weeks—and after several other scenes have been filmed—before Scene 2 is finally in front of the camera. Now we must see the man holding the key in his right hand as he comes through the door, and holding the newspaper, folded exactly as it was on the outside, under his left arm.

Therefore, when breaking down your script, you should make a conspicuous note at Scene 2 that the man must have the key in his right hand and the newspaper properly folded under his left arm as he comes through the door. By the same token, if Scene 2 is shot before Scene 1, it is still direct continuity, and these details will have to match when shooting Scene 1.

Here's another situation. The script reads: 1. INT. BEDROOM—DAY. A maid enters carrying a bowl of fresh flowers. As she crosses the room and places the flowers on a table, we see a person asleep in the bed. The maid opens the drapes partially, then exits.

During the course of Scenes 2 and 3, in other locales, it is revealed in dialogue that the sleeping person in the bedroom was murdered while the house was unattended, and the body wasn't discovered for several days. And in Scene 4 the script reads that the dead body is being removed from the room on an ambulance gurney.

Now let us suppose that the filming of Scene 4 was scheduled for the first morning of the shooting schedule. The bedroom would be furnished as per the action described in Scene 1: flowers on the table and drapes partially drawn. But here in Scene 4, the flowers would understandably be *wilted* (after a time lapse of several days).

Later the same day, or days later, Scene 1 is scheduled for filming. According to the script, the maid enters with the bowl of *fresh* flowers, places it on the table, opens the closed drapes to the position seen in Scene 4, then exits. Of course, the bowl of fresh flowers and the wilted ones we saw in Scene 4 must match exactly. The principle of direct continuity still rules, even though a time lapse occurred. The rationale is this: inasmuch as the house was unattended between Scene 1 and Scene 4, nothing in the bedroom could have been changed during the interim. Be especially attentive to details when a scene that takes place later in the story is filmed before the earlier scene.

Indirect continuity occurs when a condition or a detail does not follow through from one scene into the next consecutive scene but carries over into a later scene. Once again (as usually happens), the later scene may be shot before the earlier one. In such cases, back-matching notes are especially critical.

Let us consider this scenario: In Scene 8, a woman places a pillbox in her purse. Dialogue indicates that she has to take a pill at a later hour. In Scenes 9 through 12, we see the woman in various locales and with different characters. Then during Scene 13, the woman reaches into her purse, finds and opens the pillbox, only to discover that there are no pills inside. You and the property department were remiss in your responsibilities. The actress is annoyed, and the director is infuriated because the time that has to be spent in reshooting the scene hikes the cost of production. But had your script been conspicuously marked at Scene 13 that the pillbox, containing pills, has to be inside the woman's purse, this embarrassing situation would have been prevented.

By preparing your script breakdown with meticulous back-matching notes to signal direct and indirect continuity, you will have no problem in shooting out of continuity. Your notations will be beacon lights that will steer you clear of mishaps.

10. Scene Count

Tally the number of scenes in the script. Every scene number in the script, including those numbers carrying A, B, C, etc., count as separate scene numbers. However, do not include in your total scene count the numbers marked (OMITTED) and those marked (STOCK SHOT).

A good way to control the scene count is to make a list of every scene number in the script. List the omitted scene numbers, but draw an X through them; also list the stock shot numbers, but mark them with an S. And remember, do not add these numbers into your total scene count (see page 33).

11. Page Count

Tally the total number of pages in the script. Every numbered page, even those repeated with an A, B, C, etc., is counted; that is, 15A, 15B, and 15C equal three pages. Starting with page 15, the total comes to four pages.

When a page number reads 44/45, it means that a deletion has been made in revisions and two pages have been combined. In this instance, your page count for 44/45 is one page.

Page count is determined by the amount of written material on a page. That is, how much space the description of business/action and dialogue takes up. For shooting purposes, the standard practice is to divide the page into eighths. Every page holds an individual total of eight eighths (8/8) within the standard margins at top and bottom. If the space is not filled, then the total for that page is the number of eighths contained in the written portion. Several pages may not total 8/8.

The breaking down of page count into denominations of eighths was devised when filmmakers realized that it was more practical and economical to shoot scenes *out of continuity*—in other words, to film several sequences in one locale concurrently, no matter when they occurred chronologically. In order to make this practice viable, it was necessary to first determine the actual number of pages that each sequence contained and then to calculate the aggregate number of hours or days it would take to shoot all those sequences.

It was found that dividing a page into eighths provided the most practical unit of measure for shooting on a day-to-day basis. Thus the innovation of the *Shooting Schedule,* which is prepared by the First Assistant Director.

NOTE: In figuring your page count, do not include the space taken up by STOCK SHOTS. It is customary to deduct 1/8 page per stock shot. For example, if three stock shots are included on one page, your total count for the contents of that page is 5/8. And if the page consists of only three stock shots, then the count for that page is zero (0).

A good way to insure an accurate page count is to make a list of each consecutive page number and record the number of eighths for each fractional page (see page 34).

12. Master-Scene Page Count

At the end of every master sequence, jot down its individual page count. A master scene may add up to only 1/8 of a page. When one page contains several master scenes, each master scene scores its own page count. For example: one scene takes up 3/8 of the page, another scene 1/8 of the page, and a third scene 4/8 of the page. The sum total of that page is 8/8. When a master scene continues for several pages and adds up to, say 22/8, the page count for that master scene translates to 2 6/8 pages (22 divided by 8). As a double-check for accuracy, add all your individual master-scene page counts; the total should be identical to your total page count for the entire script, and to the total shown in the Shooting Schedule.

13. Continuity Synopsis/One Line

Prepare a continuity synopsis of the entire script. This record, sometimes called the *One Line,* constitutes a composite of the script breakdown. Listed are scene numbers and the locales (sets) of each sequence, a terse description of the action in the scene, the time elements of day or night, the chronological time lapses, the page count of each separate master scene, and the names of the characters who appear in each sequence (see page 35).

14. Wardrobe Outline*

Prepare a wardrobe outline form. This record is for your personal use. It need not be submitted to the wardrobe departments (men's and women's). However, it is advisable to confer with them and coordinate your notes with theirs as to when costume changes will occur.

The wardrobe departments have their own methods of preparing wardrobe plots. They are totally responsible for seeing that the actors are dressed in the correct garments and articles of clothing at the start of every scene or part of a scene.

15. Script Revisions

Incorporate all the script revisions into your original script as quickly as possible. Invariably, constant changes are made in the script—before and even during principal photography. Every revised page is dated and put through in a color different from the previous ones. Generally, the rotation is: white for the original, followed by blue, pink, yellow, green, goldenrod, then back to white. Some companies may vary this color routine.

Instead of revised pages, you may sometimes receive a memorandum from the production office that reads as follows:

PLEASE NOTE:
Elmer and Alice Lester should be changed to:
ELMER and *ADELE NESTOR*
Mark scripts accordingly.

Now you must go through the entire script and change "Alice" to "Adele" and "Lester" to "Nestor" on every page where these names appear. Most important, you must go through the dialogue with a fine-tooth comb to see if any of the other characters mention the names. You must personally communicate with the actors and alert them to the changes before they study and memorize the wrong names.

Also make sure that the correct names are printed on doors or desk plaques or wherever else the names might appear. Stage sets and props are often prepared in advance of shooting.

---

* The Wardrobe Outline form suggested in this book is a practical record-keeper that has proved highly efficient. It automatically provides a quick double-check on all the scene numbers that occur in each time lapse of the story. Furthermore, you have on one page the complete wardrobe description of every actor and actress who appears in the listed sequences, together with the dates on which the scenes were shot. (See Chapter 7, pages 114–116).

When you receive revised pages, heed the following instructions:

☐ Immediately transfer all your notations from the original script pages to the revised pages.

☐ Revise your Continuity Synopsis/One Line (if affected) to conform with the new version of the script.

☐ Correct your Scene Count and Page Count to reflect any deletions or additions.

☐ Do not discard previous pages after receiving revised pages. File them numerically for reference. There is a good reason for this: occasionally, the director will want to see, or will even prefer, an earlier version. In all probability, you will be the only person on the set who has a complete file of every revised page—so you will be a heroine or a hero.

16. Special Report Forms

Prepare the various report forms you will need during production (see Appendix C).

DAILY CONTINUITY LOG is your personal control sheet.

DAILY EDITOR'S LOG is given daily to the film editor.

DAILY PROGRESS REPORT is given daily to the second assistant director.

These forms are not supplied by production companies. You will have to furnish your own. It's advisable to photocopy a supply of each form for future use.

Some companies may require that you use their particular forms. If you have devised an efficient formula for a script breakdown, you can readily adapt it to any prescribed forms.

SAMPLE SCRIPT BREAKDOWN

The following pages contain the sample script breakdown of the teleplay presented at the beginning of this chapter, and memoranda of essential data that you should have with you for ready reference when you attend the production meeting—e.g., the Story Chronology/Time Breakdown, Scene Count, Page Count, Continuity Synopsis, and Wardrobe Outline.

Refer to the script breakdown. Observe the underscoring of master scene captions, names of characters and their distinguishing marks, overt actions, and special details of props and makeup; also, notations of direct continuity details, story time lapses, lines separating the master scenes, and master-scene page count.

ACT ONE

N-1

FADE IN:

1. EXT. SEAN'S FRONT DOOR - NIGHT

It is late and <u>dark.</u> SEAN comes up with a <u>suitcase</u> and
a <u>flight bag</u>. He is tired. He <u>unlocks the door</u> and
enters. He is wearing a <u>Hawaiian shirt</u> and slacks.   1/8

2. INT. SEAN'S LIVING ROOM - NIGHT *keys*
    suitcase

The <u>lights are out</u>. <u>Sean</u> enters. He yawns. He <u>is tired</u>
and wants to go right to bed. He sets down his <u>bag.</u> then,
as he heads toward the bedroom, he <u>takes off shirt</u> and
casually tosses it onto a chair or sofa. He <u>enters the</u>
<u>bedroom</u>.   1/8

3. INT. SEAN'S BEDROOM - NIGHT *(lite change)*

no shirt
The <u>lights are out</u>. <u>Sean</u> enters, <u>kicks off his shoes</u>
and <u>slides out of his pants</u>. Down to his shorts, he
sighs, yawns, then <u>slides into bed</u>, stretching out.
After a beat, a <u>female arm</u> comes lovingly <u>across his</u>
<u>chest</u> and a sweet, female voice says...

                    CELIA'S VOICE (O.S.)
              I love you...

4. WIDER ANGLE

Sean's head snaps toward the voice. He finds himself
nose to nose with a lovely young bride, <u>CELIA.</u> She
gasps. <u>Sean reacts</u>.

                         SEAN
              What the...!

                         CELIA
                    (screams)
              Ahhh...!

She <u>grabs the blankets</u> up around her.

5. ANOTHER ANGLE

<u>DAVE</u>, the groom, bursts in <u>from the bathroom</u>. He wears
a <u>bathrobe</u>. <u>Light comes in</u> from the bathroom.   6/8

                              (CONTINUED)

Figure 2.2

2.

N-1

5 (Cont.)

                    DAVE
            Baby, what is it!

6.   ANGLE ON SEAN

      He is halfway out of bed, still not certain what this is all
      about. He whips his head around to look towards the new voice.
      It has all happened in a split second. We FREEZE FRAME
      catching him in an awkward position, halfway out of bed.

                                          CUT TO: 3/8

                                                                 N-1+

7.   INT. SEAN'S LIVING ROOM - NIGHT (LATER THAT NIGHT)

      Sean, Celia and Dave are there in robes. MOE is there in
      uniform. Dave is holding his arm protectively around Celia.

                    MOE
            You wanna press charges, Doc?

                    DAVE
            What do you mean? He attacked
            my wife.

                    MOE
                (to Sean)
            Sorry, Doc...it's my duty to
            inform you of your rights.

                    SEAN
            I didn't attack her. I just got
            in bed with her.

8.   ANGLE ON FRONT DOOR
                          keys
      MRS. GRUBER lets herself in. Celia comes up to her.

                    CELIA
            Mrs. Gruber, thank goodness. Will
            you tell them you rented it to us?
            They don't believe us.

                    GRUBER
                (sees Sean)
            What are you doing here?

                    SEAN
            I live here.

                                       (CONTINUED)   6/8

3

8 (Cont.)   N-It

> GRUBER
> You weren't supposed to be
> back for a week.

> SEAN
> Well, I'm back now and I got
> mugged in my own bed.

> MOE
> (to Dave)
> You have the right to remain
> silent. You have the right to
> seek counsel.

> DAVE
> Officer, who rented this place
> to us.

> SEAN
> (to Gruber)
> You rented my apartment without
> my permission?

> MOE
> (to Gruber)
> You have the right to remain
> silent...

> SEAN
> Moe, will you shut up.

> GRUBER
> Dr. Jamison, if you'd just once
> listen to reason. It is my property
> and this young couple is on their
> honeymoon.

> CELIA
> And our reservations fell through.

> DAVE
> I told you. The hotels are packed.

> GRUBER
> I found them sitting on a bench...
> on their wedding night. You said
> you'd be away, so, being a romantic
> person, I let them stay here.

> SEAN
> For a modest fee, no doubt.

(CONTINUED)

30

8 (Cont. 1)   H-1+

                    GRUBER
          Just a breakage deposit.
               (trying to explain this)
          Well, I was just thinking about
          the night of my third wedding.
          Mario was a gymnast.

                    CELIA
               (tearfully)
          What are we going to do?

                    DAVE
          I guess we'll have to leave.

                    SEAN
               (relenting)
          Well, no. You can't leave in
          the middle of the night. I'll
          sleep on the sofa. You kids can
          have the bedroom.

     There is silence as <u>bride and groom exchange glances.</u>
     They obviously don't want Sean so close by.

                    SEAN
               (getting the message)
          Okay, I'll find someplace.

                    GRUBER
               (quickly)
          There's no room at my place.

                    SEAN
          I wouldn't trust you, anyway.

                    MOE
          Doesn't anybody want to be informed
          of their rights?

                                      DISSOLVE: 6/8
     _____

9.   INT. RECEPTION ROOM - DAY   (NEXT MORNING)   D-2

     <u>PUNI</u> adjusts some <u>flowers in a vase,</u> <u>picks up the vase</u> and
     starts with it <u>towards Sean's office.</u> <u>DR. CHAFFEE</u> enters.

                    CHAFFEE
          Good morning.

                    PUNI
          Morning, Dr. Chaffee.

                                      (CONTINUED)   3/8

5.   D-2

9 (Cont.)

> CHAFFEE
> Puni, I've told you and told you...
> stop putting flowers around.

> PUNI
> But Doctor, this is Hawaii.

> CHAFFEE
> I don't care. They're full of
> pollen. They'll make my patients
> sneeze.

He exits into the corridor. Puni looks after him and
makes a face.

> PUNI
> Yankee, go home.

CUT TO: 3/8

---

10.   INT. SEAN'S OFFICE - DAY (MORNING)   D-2

Puni enters and sets the vase of flowers on his desk.

11.   ANOTHER ANGLE

Sean, wearing a rumpled sport shirt and pants, is stirring
on the sofa where he apparently has spent the night.

> PUNI
> Dr. Jamison, what are you doing
> here?

> SEAN
> (stretches, feels back)
> I've been asking myself that all
> night.
> (rubs back again)
> Ohhh...
> (gets up)

> PUNI
> But, Doctor, why couldn't you
> sleep in your own bed?

> SEAN
> It was two against one...

Puni reacts.

CUT TO: 7/8

32

STORY CHRONOLOGY/TIME BREAKDOWN

TITLE:_____

SCENE NOS.	TIME
1-6	1ST NITE
7-8	LATER 1ST NITE
9-11	2ND DAY
12-14	LATER 2ND DAY
15-18	2ND NITE
19-30	LATER 2ND NITE
31-35	3RD DAY
36-39	4TH DAY
40-40	LATER 4TH DAY
41-44	4TH NITE
45-59	LATER 4TH NITE
60-60	5TH DAY
61-63	5TH NITE
	(END)

The above reflects the scene numbers of the complete script.

SCENE COUNT

TITLE: _____

1	21	41	61
2	~~22~~	42	62
3	23	43	63
4	24/S	44	
5	25	45	TOTAL 60
6	26	46	STOCK 2
7	27	47	
8	28	48	
9	29	~~49~~	
10	30	49A	
11	31	50	
12	32	51	
13	33	52	
13A	34	53	
14	~~35~~	54	
15	35A	55	
16	36/S	56	
17	37	~~57~~	
18	38	58	
19	39	59	
20	40	60	

The above reflects the scene count of the complete script.

34

PAGE COUNT

TITLE: _____

1	21	FULL PAGES	33
2	22	PART PAGES	
3	23	8|31	3 7/8
4	24	TOTAL	36 7/8
√	24A - 3		
6	25		
7	26		
8	27 - 4		
9	28		
10	29		
11	30 - √		
12	31		
13	32		
14	33		
15 - 7	33A - 4		
16	34		
17	35√		
18 - 4	36		
19	37 - 2		
20	38		
20A - 2			

The above reflects the page count of the complete script.

CONTINUITY SYNOPSIS/ONE LINE

TITLE _____   PROD. NO. _____

DIRECTOR _____   DATE _____

SCENE NOS.	SET	DESCRIPTION	D/N	PAGES	CHARACTERS
1	EXT SEAN DOOR	SEAN W/BAGS UNLOCKS DOOR, GOES INSIDE	N-1	1/8	SEAN
2	SEAN LIVING RM	SEAN ENTERS FROM EXT. DROPS HAT + BAG, EXITS TO BEDROOM	N-1	1/8	SEAN
3, 4, 5, 6	SEAN BEDROOM	SEAN ENTERS, DISROBES, GETS INTO BED, CELIA IN BED. DAVE BURSTS IN FROM BATHROOM. FREEZE ON SEAN	N-1	1	SEAN CELIA DAVE
7, 8	SEAN LIVING RM	GROUP ARGUE. SEAN, CELIA, DAVE IN ROBES; MOE IN UNIFORM WANTS TO PRESS CHARGES. GRUBER ENTERS TELLS SHE RENTED HOUSE TO HONEYMOON COUPLE. SEAN RELENTS, WILL SLEEP ON SOFA	LATER N-1	2 4/8	SEAN CELIA DAVE MOE GRUBER
9	RECEPTION RM	PUNI BRINGING FLOWERS TO SEAN'S OFFICE. CHAFFEE ENTERS, COMPLAINS OF POLLEN	D-2	5/8	PUNI CHAFFEE
10, 11	SEAN'S OFFICE	PUNI ENTERS WITH FLOWERS FINDS SEAN ASLEEP ON SOFA	D-2	5/8	PUNI SEAN

WARDROBE OUTLINE

TITLE _____   Time Breakdown __N-1__

Scene Nos.	Sets	Date Shot
1	EXT SEAN FRONT DOOR	
2	SEAN LIVING ROOM	
3, 4	⎰ SEAN BEDROOM	
5	⎨ ANGLE BATHROOM	
6	⎱ SEAN BEDROOM	

CHARACTERS

SEAN _____   CELIA _____

DAVE _____

WARDROBE OUTLINE

TITLE _____   Time Breakdown _N-1 (LATER)_

Scene Nos.   Sets   Date Shot
_7, 8_   _SEAN LIVING ROOM_   _____

_____   _____   _____
_____   _____   _____
_____   _____   _____
_____   _____   _____
_____   _____   _____
_____   _____   _____

CHARACTERS

SEAN   _CELIA_

DAVE   _GRUBER_

MOE

WARDROBE OUTLINE

TITLE _____   Time Breakdown _D-2_

Scene Nos.	Sets	Date Shot
9	RECEPTION ROOM	
10, 11	SEAN OFFICE	

CHARACTERS

SEAN   PUN I

CHAFFEE

Every script breakdown mandates all the exacting procedures outlined in the previous pages. Each step applies whether the company is shooting a half-hour television show or a four-hour feature film.

Up to this point, you have learned the first phase involved in the craft of script supervising and film continuity: How to Read and Break Down a Script. And I shall end this segment with the caution BEWARE THE 5 P's: *POOR PREPARATION PRODUCES POOR PERFORMANCE.*

When you have the utmost confidence in the preciseness of your script breakdown, you can then focus your full attention on the other important functions that come within the scope of your responsibility in the preeminent role of continuity supervisor.

3

Prior to Principal Photography

PREPARATION TIME

Before the start of principal photography, there is a period known as *preparation (prep) time*. Key personnel are given the then-final version of the script and put on salary. Each crew member prepares the script according to his or her specific job. The number of days or weeks allotted for prep time depends on the complexity of the script, the number of scheduled shooting days, and the budget.

During this time period, you will be conscientiously preparing your script—that is, breaking it down according to the procedures previously outlined. The better you have prepared your script, the greater control you will have during the hectic days of shooting *out of continuity*.

THE PRODUCTION MEETING*

Before filming begins, a production meeting is held, usually in the producer's office. All key personnel attend with their respective script breakdowns. Page by page, the business/action elements of the entire script

---

* If the production meeting and/or scheduled rehearsal days coincide with your preparation days, it is advisable that you include in your *Deal Memo* (negotiations with respect to employment conditions) that you will receive additional compensation for those days, apart from prep time.

are read and discussed. First the producer and director make known how they perceive the written script interpreted on film. Then the other members of the group discuss the technical and practical elements relevant to their own respective crafts. If anyone brings up a foreseeable difficulty in achieving on film what the author has written, the problem is resolved and the executives decide whether to alter, replace, or eliminate the questionable elements. These changes will appear in the revised final shooting script.

If, in the process of breaking down your script, you found a discrepancy or an inaccuracy that was not brought up by the others, you must bring this to attention before the meeting adjourns so that all concerned can make the necessary corrections. If you do not attend the production meeting, you will have to convey your findings individually to every person whose work may be affected. Before you do so, however, first clear your findings with the director. Since you do not know what transpired at the meeting, it may very well be that your question was fully answered.

It is always to your advantage to attend production meetings. Here you will be privileged to the director's interpretation of the script in terms of details that are not always spelled out by the writers. You should carefully annotate your script with the proposed changes, if any. It may happen that a scene will be scheduled for shooting before the revised pages come from the production office. In that case, your script notes may make it possible for the company to start shooting without delay, because you will be in a position to inform the director, and any others who are concerned, of the consequential issues that were resolved at the production meeting.

THE SHOOTING SCHEDULE

A few days before the start of filming, you will receive the Shooting Schedule (see Figure 3.1), which has been prepared by the first assistant director. This is the official document that lists the order in which scenes will be shot. It contains a concise description of each master sequence with its corresponding scene numbers and page count. The schedule shows the total number of pages to be shot each day, lists the actors who perform in each sequence, lists all the required props and special effects, and notes any extraordinary items called for in the script. In the event that shooting will take place at an outside location, the schedule notes the address of the site; if the address has not been confirmed by the time the schedule has been completed, the letters TBA (to be announced) will appear.

It is important to promptly compare the Shooting Schedule with your Continuity Synopsis/One Line to make sure that all the elements are in accord. Any differences should be checked with the first assistant director without delay. The tally of your daily reports must correspond to the shooting schedule's data.

SHOOTING SCHEDULE

SIMON & SIMON

Prod. No. 64413   Director: GERALD McRANEY
Title: "Simon Says 'Goodbye'"   Ass't. Director: KEVIN CORCORAN
Start: 1/16/89   Unit Manager: PAUL CAJERO
Finish.   1/24/89 (Camera Days - 7)

DAY/DATE	DESCRIPTION OF SET	CAST & ATMOS	PAGES	VEHICLES LIVESTOCK PROPS	DAY or NITE
DAY 1 MONDAY 1/16/89 BEVERLY BOULEVARD, L.A.	EXT. PHONE BOOTH NEAR POLICE STATION Scs. 11 pt,12 pt. Dolph tells Holridge that the Simons are researching "Terry Adamson."	DOLPH 4-standins w/cars ATMOS 4-uniformed cops w/change for gallery 14-street types w/change for gallery (2-w/cars)	2/8	PROPS: Phone VEHICLES: 2-cop cars CAMERA: 2-cameras SET DEC: Pay phone	D-2
	EXT. PHONE NEAR RESTAURANT Scs. 23A,24 pt. Outside restaurant, Dolph calls Holridge.	DOLPH A.J. ? RICK ? ELISE ? JEFF ? 4-standins w/cars ATMOS 14-street types (2-w/cars)	2/8	VEHICLES: Camaro ?	D-3
	INT. RESTAURANT Scs. 22,22A Over lunch Elise tells the Simons about "Terry."	A.J. RICK ELISE JEFF 4-standins w/cars ATMOS 1-busboy 1-waiter 6-customers 8-street types (2-w/cars)	2-7/8	PROPS: Food & drink VEHICLES: Camaro	D-3

(1ST DAY CONTINUED)

Reprinted through courtesy of Universal Television

Figure 3.1

THE CALL SHEET/SHOOTING CALL

On the day before the first day of filming, the second assistant director will distribute a *Call Sheet* (some companies use the term *Shooting Call;* see Figure 3.2). This document lists all the scenes that will be shot that day, as outlined in the Shooting Schedule. It also stipulates the hours at which all personnel (cast and crew) must report to the sound stage or location. A new Call Sheet will be distributed for each shooting day.

Once again, if you discover any discrepancies between your records and the Call Sheet, check these out with the first assistant director and make the necessary corrections in your records.

PRETIMING SCRIPTS

Some companies want to have a general idea of the playing time (*picture-running time*) of a script before the start of photography. Proficiency at calculating picture-running time entails skillful timing of the dialogue and the business/action in each scene. It is advantageous to possess an innate sense of dramaturgy, although that talent can be acquired with experience.

At best, the total time can only be approximated. There is no way of knowing the pace at which the cast of characters will speak (an actor may decide to stylize his role with a stutter); there is no way of knowing how the director's stage technique will pace the performance; one can only guess how much time to allow for traveling vehicles, car chases, pregnant pauses, or panoramic scenery. The accuracy of your guesswork is the measure of your proficiency as a timer of scripts.

There is still another complicating factor: constant revisions. Every revised page invariably alters the original timing. Despite the inexactitude of the result, some companies still insist on a general (if vague) idea of the playing time of a script before the start of photography.

It is inadvisable for you to attempt the pretiming of scripts before you have had ample experience as a continuity supervisor. When you have developed a good aptitude for figuring picture-running time, you might undertake the formidable task of pretiming scripts. Here is a practical suggestion: When organizing your script breakdown, practice timing the interior and exterior master sequences. Keep a record of these timings and compare them to the actual picture time when the scenes are filmed. See how close your timing comes to the picture time.

When you acquire professional skill in pretiming scripts, it will bring you extra remuneration, because this work is separate from prep time. The number of hours it takes to render a complete scene-by-scene timing estimate depends on the length of the script and the complexity of the story. Payment for these assignments is negotiable.

```
SHOOTING CALL                         FILM
UNIVERSAL CITY STUDIOS, INC
Due to Extreme Fire Hazard. Please Be Careful Smoking. Use Butt Cans.          Unit        1   Day of Shooting
```

Production		No.	Director	
"SIMON SAYS GOODBYE"		64413	G. MCRANEY	

Series		Date	
SIMON & SIMON - 1 HR. TV		MONDAY, 1/16/89	

Art Director	Shooting Call Time	Condition Of Call
CRONE	7:30AM	R/S

Set Dresser			
DECINCES		[X] REPORT TO LOCATION	[ ] BUS TO LOCATION

CREW CALL: 630A @ LOC

PAGES	SET DESCRIPTION	SC. NO.	D/N	LOCATION
2/8	EXT. PHONE NR.POLICE STA. (DOLPH,ATMOS.)	11PT.,12PT.	D2	AUTHENIC CAFE 7605 BEVERLY BL.
	-1/2 BLOCK MOVE-			
2/8	EXT. PHONE NR.RESTAURANT (DOLPH,ATMOS.-CAMARO)	23A,24A	D3	
2-7/8	INT. RESTAURANT (AJ,RICK,ELISE,JEFF,ATMOS.)	22,22A	D3	
	-1/2 BLOCK MOVE-			
3/8	INT. ART GALLERY (RICK,DOLPH,ATMOS.)	42A,42C,43	D4	SAXON LEE GALLERY, 7525
2-5/8	INT. ART GALLERY (RICK,HOLRIDGE,DOLPH,ATMOS.)	44,45	D4	BEVERLY BLVD.
6/8	INT. ART GALLERY/LEVEL 2 (HOLRIDGE,DOLPH,ATMOS.)	46	D4	
2/8	INT. ART GALLERY (HOLRIDGE,DOLPH O.S.,ATMOS.)	11PT.,12PT.	D2	

ALL CALLS SUBJECT TO CHANGE BY ASSISTANT DIRECTOR AT WRAP

CAST AND BITS	CHARACTERS		RPT TO	CALL TIME	ON SET
JAMESON PARKER*	(NEW)	A.J.SIMON	PU@HOME	LOC @ 715A	8A
GERALD MCRANEY*	(NEW)	RICK SIMON	PU@HOME	LOC @ 715A	8A
GERARD PRENDERGAST	(NEW)	DOLPH	LOC	630A	730A
CATHERINE MACNEAL	(NEW)	ELISE	LOC	615A	8A
RANDY HALL	(NEW)	JEFF	LOC	7A	8A
BRIAN PATRICK CLARKE	(NEW)	HOLDRIGE	LOC	10A	1045A
BILL BURTON	(NEW)	UTILITY STUNT	LOC	630A	W/N

NOTES: PARKING LOT FOR CREW DOES NOT OPEN BEFORE 6AM.
        ALL COMPANY - CAUTION - FILMING IN ART GALLERY WITH HIGH
        VALUE ART WORK - PLEASE BE CAREFUL WHEN WORKING NEXT TO
        ART WORK.
*ND BREAKFAST PROVIDED

ATMOSPHERE AND STANDINS	RPT TO	CALL TIME	ON SET
4 SI'S (BARTLETT,JEPSEN,MACE,DILLEY)W/CARS	LOC	630A	W/N
4 UNIFORM POLICE (3M,1F) W/OWN CLOTHES FOR GALLERY	LOC	630A	W/N
14 PEDESTRIANS W/CHNG FOR GALLERY- 2 W/AUTO-INCL.1 BUSBOY (M),1 WAITER (M)	LOC	630A	W/N
3 CONTEST WINNERS-WAIVERS	PU @ 9A	915A	W/N
1 MINOR (M)		9A	W/N

***************************** ADVANCE *****************************
TUES., 1/17:
INT. ART GALLERY   SC 24PT.,51PT.,52,1PT.,2PT.,3,
                              54,55
EXT. PKG LOT NR GALLERY   SC 4

Reprinted through courtesy of Universal Television

Figure 3.2

PRODUCTION REQUIREMENTS

UNIVERSAL STUDIOS

FILM

Production	"SIMON SAYS GOODBYE"

Director	Production No.	Shooting Time	Date
G. MCRANEY	64413	7:30AM	MONDAY, 1/16/89

Set	Location	Phone
# 6 EXT. PHONE BOOTH NR POLICE STA	7605 BEVERLY BL.	(818)939-4626
# 52 INT. PHONE BOOTH NR RESTAURANT		
# 51 INT. ART GALLERY	7525 BEVERLY BL.	(818)993-5282
#		
#		

No.	CAMERA		Time	No.	TECHNICAL		Time	No.	LOCATION		Time
	Cam:			1	Key Grip	BEAM	554A	X	Permits	AS REQ.	
2	Panavision	PKG	TRK	1	2nd Grip	SLEMMONS	618A	2	Police	BDYGRDS	630A
1	ARRI-BACKUP		TRK	2	Co Grips		630A	1	Firewarden		730A
	Zoom For:				Co Grips			2	Police/Cycles		545A
1	Dir. of Photog.	MARTINEL	554A	2	Crane Oper.	VESPER	618A		POLICE		
2	Operator	BETTCHER	630A		Crane			1*	Flag Person	LOC @	6A
2	1st Assistant	MENONI+1	618A	1	Crab Dolly	FISHER	TRK		Set Watch	(*CAR WATCH)	
1	2nd Assistant		618A	1		PEE-WEE	TRK		Night Watch		
	Camera Mech.				Greens Person				Uniform Police		
	SOUND			1	CSE Setup		630A		Studio Firefighter		
1	Mixer	RIGGINS	630A		Painter				HOSPITAL		
1	Recorder	DUNN	630A		Propmaker			1	1st Aid		630A
1	Boom Oper.	MITCHELL	618A	2	Special Effects	EVANS +1	630A				
	Cable Person				Effects				TRANSPORTATION	Drv.	
	Playbk. Oper.				Sing. Dr. Rm.			1	Driver Capt.	COORD. D	O/C
	VTR Oper.							1	Co/Capt.	CAPT. D	4.8
X	Booms	AS ORD.	TRK		Dbl. Dr. Rm.				Mini		
X	Mikes	"	TRK		Quad				Maxi		
X	RF Mikes	"	TRK						Sta. Wgn		
X	Mixer/Nagra	"	TRK		Schoolrm.			1	MAXI-PROD/WD	D	5.5
14	Walkie Talkie	PU*DEPT.	W/N		Heat Stg. #				Buses		
2	Megaphone	AS ORD.	TRK		Heaters				Grip/Elec/Gen		
6	CHARGES BATTS.		W/N		ELECTRICAL			1	Duz All	#460 D	5.3
1	MOTOROLA REPEAT		TRK	1	Gaffer	HARMON	554A				
	SPECIAL PHOTOGRAPHY			1	2nd Elect.	KENNEDY	618A	1	Grip	#359 D	5.3
	Process DP			4	Lamp Opers.		630A	1	Elec.	#357 D	5.3
	Matte Supvr.			1	Lamp Opers.	BARR	618A	1	Generator	D	5.3
	Matte Crew				Gen. Oper.			1	CAM/SND #360	D	5.3
	Moviola & Oper.				Generator				Prop		
	Grip				Wind Mach. Oper.			1D	San. Wgn 7 Rms.		6.0
	Head Proj.				Wind Mach.				San. Wgn Rms.		
	Projectionist				Battery Person				Powder Trk.		
	Proj. Equip.				Batteries						
					Air Cond.				Util. Trk.		
					Work Lights			1	4 X 4	C/CAB D	4.8
	STILL PHOTO				Wigs/Phone			1	MU TRLR		TOWED
	Still Photog.				PROPERTY			1	Ward.	TRLR	TOWED
	Still Eq. P/U			2	Property Mstr.	BINKLEY	630A		Insert Car		
	FOOD SERVICE			1	Asst. Prop	HALL	630A	1	Car Carrier	D	5.3
X	Caterer	MICHELSO	6A		Benches For #						
	Breakfasts				Makeup Tables			1	Jeep		TOWED
X	Walkng Breakfasts	PER A.D.	W/N		Ward Racks						
X	Gals Coffee X	Doz. Donuts		X	Chairs	DIR/CAST TRK			Water Wgn		
90	Lunches	20@12P	1230P					1	Motor Hm. For PARKER	D	W/N
	Dinners				MAKEUP						
	Suppers			1	Makeup Artist	DAWSON	612A	1	Motor Hm. For MCRANE	D	W/N
	UNIT MANAGER			1	Extra MU	HOUSE	6A				
1	Script Supvr.	LOOMIS	6A		Extra MU				Mechanic		
	Animal Handler				Body MU						
	Wrangler			1	Hairstylist	POST	6A		Pict. Equip.		
	Livestock				Extra Hair			2	SDPD CARS		
1	TEACHER-STRANGM		9A		Extra Hair			1	AJ'S CAMARO		
1	DIALOG COACH-		630A		COSTUME						
	SNYDER			1	Mens Cstmr	LANTZ	6A				
	MUSIC				Extra Mens			X	PU CONTEST		9A
	Piano Player			1	Ladies Cstmr	WING	6A		WINNERS @		
	Music Rep				Extra Ladies						
	Sideline Mus.										

DEPARTMENT	MISCELLANEOUS & SPECIAL INSTRUCTIONS
PROPS:	PHOTO OF YOUNGER HOLDRIGE.
PROD.	INFORM CENTRAL OF LOOK-A-LIKES FOR DOLPH.
SET DEC.	2 PAY PHONES

Assistant Director	CORCORAN/STOUT/THOMP	Unit Mgr	PAUL CAJERO	Approved	RALPH SARIEGO

Reprinted through courtesy of Universal Television

Figure 3.2 *(continued)*

PRODUCTION PERSONNEL

Before we proceed with further specifics of the continuity supervisor's craft, let us get acquainted with the members of the production staff with whom you will have occasion to interact during the course of a shoot.

Executive Producer is the person who has brought together all the creative and financial elements in the making of a motion picture or television film; presides over the production.

Producer (also known as *Line Producer*) functions under the executive producer or is the person assigned by the studio to administer and oversee the production.

Associate Producer is an assistant to the producer; handles certain administrative operations.

Director is responsible for creating all the dramatic and technical components that transform a script into a motion picture; participates with the actors in interpreting their roles; is the ultimate authority on the set.

Production Manager is in charge of all business affairs concerning preparation, preproduction, production, and postproduction operations of the company; oversees the budget and hires the crew.

Unit Manager serves under the production manager; is responsible for the efficient operation of a company shoot that is on location.

Assistant Director (AD) is the person who functions as the first assistant to the director; composes the *production board* and devises the Shooting Schedule for the entire production; is responsible for expediting each day's agenda; provides everything necessary for the director; is responsible for maintaining smooth working conditions and a harmonious atmosphere on the stage; answers to the production manager.

Second Assistant Director serves under the AD (first assistant director); handles all the clerical details; distributes the daily Call Sheet; is responsible for giving work calls to the cast and other personnel; keeps time cards of the cast and crew in accordance with guild and union rates and regulations; gathers daily reports from all departments and turns them over to the production office.

Director of Photography (DP) (also called *Cinematographer* or *Cameraman*) is the chief camera person; consults with the director to effect the artistic aspects of lighting and camera placement that best reflect the style and ambience of the story.

Camera Operator is the person who physically operates the camera and is responsible for properly composing and framing the subjects being filmed, under the supervision of the director of photography (DP).

Camera First Assistant (also called *Focus Puller*) installs (threads) the magazine of film into the camera and also removes it after the footage has been shot; focuses the lenses during filming.

Camera Second Assistant is responsible for loading the raw film into the magazine and then unloading the exposed film into cans; functions as the *Slate Operator* (sometimes referred to as the *Clapper*) during shooting; keeps record of all the camera shots and takes, printed and unprinted; checks prints of slate and take numbers with the continuity supervisor; turns in a daily report to the second assistant director.

Film Editor determines the creative approach to editing the content of the film and crafts the most effective shots into proper sequence and dramatic continuity.

Assistant Film Editor (also known as *Cutter*) is the film editor's chief aid; assembles all the processed film (dailies); splices (joins together) the cut pieces of film and assembles them on reels for viewing in a screening room.

Sound Mixer operates the sound panel (trade name, Nagra); balances and controls the recording of the dialogue and all sound tracks during filming; keeps record and checks the printed slate and take numbers with the continuity supervisor; turns in a daily report to the second assistant director.

Boom Operator handles the boom microphone, an apparatus that picks up all the dialogue and sound that takes place during the shooting of a scene and transmits it to a recorder; is responsible for the placement of microphones (mikes) in the set and on the bodies of performers as required.

Property Master furnishes all the props (special articles) called for in the script; attends to these articles when handled by the performers, or places props as set dressing.

Assistant Property Master helps the property master; supervises the props that are used during shooting.

Production Designer is the key person in the art department; consults with the producer and director in developing the artistic concept for the production; prepares blueprints; employs personnel for the art department.

Art Director (also called *Set Designer*) is on the staff of the production designer; designs original sets or recreates the sets depicted in the script; provides storyboards (see *Production Illustrator*), which assist the director in visualizing the stage sets and the characters' positions in them.

Production Illustrator is on the staff of the art director; creates *storyboards:* illustrations that depict the action written in the script.

Set Decorator is on the staff of the art department; handles the purchasing or renting of furnishings for the sets as conceived by the art director; arranges the furniture and decorations in the set.

Makeup Artist attends to the general cosmetic needs of the actors and actresses during filming; creates distinctive makeup as called for in the script (e.g., period images and science-fiction character illusions).

Hair Stylist (also called *Hairdresser*) is responsible for grooming actresses' and actors' hair during filming; styles and dresses the coiffures as specified in the script, e.g., wigs and hairdos for period pictures.

Costume Designer creates the style and personality of the garments worn by the performers, as depicted in the script.

Men's Costumer is responsible for procuring, fitting, and maintaining the wardrobe for male performers.

Women's Costumer is responsible for procuring, fitting, and maintaining the wardrobe for female performers.

Stand-in is a person who "stands in" for a principal performer while lights and equipment are being adjusted after a scene has been staged by the director. (The stars are thus spared the discomfort of standing under hot lights for any length of time.)

Double is a person who resembles a featured performer and substitutes for that performer when dangerous and risky action is involved; or when the performer's actual appearance is unessential, such as in long shots of the person walking, running, or mingling in a crowd. (Sometimes a double is also a *Stuntperson*.)

Stuntperson is one who performs actions and feats that cannot be executed by, or would endanger, the principal actors, e.g., car crashes, leaps from buildings, vicious fights.

Extras (also called *The Atmosphere*) are actors or industry professionals who work in scenes without speaking; they appear in crowds, in street scenes, as diners in a restaurant, as dancers in a ballroom, as soldiers on a battlefield, as audience members in a theater.

Bit Player is an actor or actress who performs small parts in a film, with or without dialogue. When a director singles out an extra and gives that person a special piece of business or some dialogue (even just one word) that extra becomes known as a bit player.

Dialogue Coach assists performers in their speaking roles; practices with actors when certain accents are required, such as those from Texas, Boston, the Deep South; practices with foreign performers to help them improve their American speech, or with American actors who need to speak with a foreign accent.

Special Effects Personnel invent, construct, and operate mechanical atmospheric simulations or any illusionary concepts (e.g., for science-fiction epics); make operable the appliances and devices that must function for the actors during the performance of a scene.

Still Photographer is a camera person who shoots still photographs of the sets and the actors for use by the makeup, wardrobe, and property departments; also shoots pictures for publicity.

Gaffer is the key electrician; knows where the power is located on any sound stage; supervises all the lighting equipment and handles the placement of lights according to the concepts of the director of photography (DP).

Grip is the key stagehand and master carpenter; keeps stage sets in working order; supervises the installation and handling of movable walls and backdrop scenery; constructs dolly tracks and camera mounts.

Best Boy (Electrical Dept.) is the first assistant to the gaffer.

Best Boy (Grip Dept.) is the first assistant to the key grip.

Dolly Grip is the person who pushes the wheeled platform on which the camera is mounted; makes directional moves called for by the action in the scene.

Electricians (also called *Lamp Operators,* sometimes referred to, facetiously, as *Juicers*) are on the staff of the gaffer's department; assist with the handling of lighting equipment and the adjustment of lights.

Cable Operator is responsible for connecting cables to the sound equipment on the set.

Generator Operator handles the apparatus that supplies electricity for the equipment used when shooting is done at outdoor locations or at any locale away from the studio.

Scenic Artist (also called *Scenic Designer*) paints the walls and scenery background (murals) in the set.

Assistant Scenic Artist repairs the damage done to walls and scenery during the shooting of a scene.

Craft Service Person is responsible for opening and closing the sound stage doors; keeps the stages clean; provides coffee and refreshments for the cast and crew; and generally does helpful jobs around the stage.

First Aid Nurse is a registered professional who administers first aid; ministers to the discomforts and minor injuries of the cast and crew; accompanies the production company when shooting on location and accompanies to the hospital anyone who sustains a major injury; makes written reports of any accidents.

Welfare Worker is the person who makes sure that babies and children are properly handled on- and off-camera, in accordance with established labor laws.

School Teacher is hired through the public education system to teach the prescribed curriculum to underage performers. Classrooms are provided on the sound stages or at the locations where filming takes place.

Animal Trainer is the person who trains animals for appearances in films.

Animal Handler is the person who takes charge of the handling of any animals used in films.

Wrangler is the person who handles the horses that work in films. (The name is sometimes applied, facetiously, to the handlers of any other species in the animal kingdom, e.g., pigs, cats, canaries, tarantulas.)

Greensperson furnishes and maintains all the plant life (natural and artificial) that is called for as set dressing—from a jungle in a corner of the sound stage to a geranium plant on a windowsill. The latter, if artificial, might be handled by the property master.

Musical Director composes or selects the music for scoring the completed film; supervises staging of musical productions.

Music Editor fits the music to the completed film.

Sound Effects Editor incorporates into the completed film all the necessary sound effects, such as off-screen door closing, telephones ringing, gun-shots, babies crying, and all sounds from special effects apparatus.

4

A Day on the Sound Stage

The continuity supervisor

as all the answers

BEFORE THE CAMERA ROLLS

The day begins with all personnel reporting to the sound stage or designated location at the times specified for them on the Daily Call Sheet.

There is no such thing as a routine day in the life of a continuity supervisor. Every moment holds something unpredictable. In the text that follows, you will get acquainted with the sights and sounds that fill a stage set before the camera starts to roll, during the rolling of the camera, and after the filming has been completed.

RIGGING THE STAGE

A preliminary step in filming procedure is *rigging the stage.* The technical crew—key grip and carpenters, key gaffer and electricians, and other stagehands—arrive earlier and rig the set. That is, they construct scaffolding and apparatus for the placement of lights and equipment required in the filming of scenes.

For a scene on a sound stage (indoors or simulated outdoors), the crew mounts overhead lights on the *scaffolds* (also called *catwalks*), and installs walls, floors, fixtures, and any called-for décor. The special effects technicians prepare in advance the apparatus that will activate any fixtures or appliances that have to be functional in the playing of a scene. They also position in advance the equipment that will create any atmospheric conditions indicated in the script.

For an indoor (INT.) scene away from the studio, the room is equipped with portable lights, and set dressing is arranged according to what is depicted in the script.

For an outdoor (EXT.) scene away from the studio, set dressing is suitably placed, any structures indicated in the script are erected, and dolly tracks are laid if needed.

When shooting is done at a location away from the studio (indoors or outdoors), all the rigging equipment—generators, lights, set furnishings, etc.—is transported via truck to the site. Also driven to the sites are trailers that house dressing rooms and washroom facilities.

THE LINEUP

When the technical crews finish the basic fittings of the set, the director of photography (DP) notifies the director and the first assistant director that the stage is ready for a *lineup,* which means the stage is ready for the camera to view the action that will take place in the *setup.* The setup is the specific area on which the camera focuses to film the action.

The first assistant director instructs the second assistant director to summon the actors to the set.

The second assistant director finds the actors, wherever they happen to be—in dressing rooms, at makeup tables, in wardrobe departments—and addresses them with "Ready on stage," "Ready on the set," "Ready for setup," "Ready for walk-through," or some other industry expression that signifies a call to action. This call to action is also heeded by the stand-ins.

As the cast approaches the set, the first assistant director shouts, "Let's have a bell!" Then the sound mixer presses a button that renders a loud ring or buzz heard throughout the sound stage or the location set. The bell alerts all personnel involved in the scene to assemble around the camera.

The director, flanked by key personnel—DP, first assistant director, gaffer, grip, property master, boom operator, set decorator, and continuity supervisor—studies the set and extemporizes how the master shot might be choreographed. Each of the craftspeople listens intently for any detail the director might mention that falls within the scope of his or her responsibility.

BLOCKING THE SET

The director sketches out the course of movements for each actor as motivated by the dialogue and written business. Without speaking the actual dialogue, the actors take their respective positions and extemporize or read from their scripts so that the *camera blocking* can be worked out.

The DP looks through the viewfinder—a small instrument hung on a cord around the neck. The viewfinder indicates the perspective that limits the *depth of field* for the stage setting. The DP watches the action and determines where to place the *key light* (the principal lamp that illuminates the set) and whether the scene will require a stationary or a moving camera.

A *moving camera* is one that is mounted on a platform with wheels, called a *dolly,* or one that has a base equipped with rubber wheels, known as a *crab dolly.* The crab dolly moves more smoothly and has greater mobility because its wheels can also slide sideways (as the crab moves).

The DP decides where to place secondary lights to achieve the most characteristic and artistic atmosphere for the scene.

The gaffer stays close to the DP for instructions on where to place the key and secondary lights. The gaffer then knows the number and dimension of the lights the set will require. In turn, these instructions are relayed to the electrical staff: the best boy and lamp operators.

The gaffer also places the lights that are to be snapped on and off during the performance. These lights may be overhead fixtures, wall fixtures, or table lamps. Such fixtures are known as *practicals,* which means they function during the scene. If a fixture in a set has to be operative during a performance, it is *practical;* if the same fixture does not play in the set, then it is *set dressing.* For instance, during a day sequence, a table lamp will be set dressing; the same lamp will be practical during a night sequence.

The key grip determines whether a wall, part of a wall, or some fixture needs to be moved into or taken out of the set, whether a dolly track has to be laid, whether a backdrop is required beyond a window for either a day or night scene. A wall that is moved in and out of a set is known as a *fly wall* or a *wild wall.*

The set decorator has already installed a few pieces of furniture and décor. The director confirms that they are suitable, or may suggest some changes.

The boom operator observes where the dialogue and action are taking place and informs the sound mixer where best to station the recorder panel. The boom operator also judges whether to use an *overhead boom* or *floor mikes* (microphones). If floor mikes are to be used, they will be placed stategically so that they are hidden from camera range. The boom and microphones record all the sound and dialogue that takes place in the set. Sometimes, when both the boom and floor mikes are not feasible, actors have to be "wired for sound." That means they are outfitted with tiny transistors (called *lavalieres*) attached invisibly to some part of their clothing. The dialogue is thus transmitted to the sound panel. This technique is customarily used when filming is done outdoors: when actors are talking while walking in a park or along a street, or while riding in a vehicle.

The property master provides all the hand props and stage props described in the script, or assures the director that they will be ready when needed.

The special effects technicians will have made ready the proper installation of all the practical fixtures called for in the scene: running water from a sink faucet or garden hose, gas burning on a stove, wood burning in a fireplace, breakaway articles, explosions, even levitations—all the contrivances conjured up by the writer. If the script indicates special weather conditions such as rain, wind, fog, or snow, the technicians will have installed the necessary equipment, ready for action.

THE WALK-THROUGH

After the set has been blocked and made ready for rehearsal, the actors *walk through* their moves as many times as the director deems necessary, to make adjustments in the blocking or to try variations that might enhance the dynamics of the scene.

The stand-ins concentrate on the actors' physical moves; they have to repeat them exactly. Customarily, every principal actor has a stand-in. Usually, the stand-ins resemble the actors somewhat physically, especially in height, as that affects their lighting.

As continuity supervisor, you participate by listening to all comments and noting on the script any proposed suggestions that deviate from the written dialogue and/or business. It is your job to continually alter the script to reflect what is being put on film.

In the course of the blocking and repeated rehearsals, you will gain insight into the dynamics of the scene. During this period, the director expresses some ideas on *coverage* (see Chapter 1, page 7). You will hear such remarks as "I want to get a two shot of Mary and Joe . . . a close-up of Robert . . . a tight three at the door . . . and an insert of the calendar." These directional instructions (see "Definitions of Industry Terms" in Chapter 8) will be important later on in the shooting, so be sure to make careful notations.

MARKING THE ACTORS

When the director and the DP are satisfied with the blocking of the scene, the DP announces, "Mark 'em." That's an instruction to the second assistant camera to place a small piece of tape or chip of wood at the feet of the actors where they stand at the start of the scene and at each stopping point of their designated moves. Then the camera assistant stretches a tape measure from the point of the camera lens to the actors' noses in each of their positions. These measurements of the distances between the subject and the camera indicate what focal-length lenses will be used during filming.

LIGHTING WITH STAND-INS

When the actors have been marked, they leave the set, and the stand-ins take their places. Then the electrical crew proceeds with the lighting, and other craftspeople work at readying the furnishings and dressings required for the set.

ACTIVITIES WHILE WAITING FOR THE SET

During the period of lighting and set preparation, the sound stage assumes an incongruous yet familiar ambience: people read "the trades" (*Hollywood Reporter* and *Daily Variety*) or newspapers, play chess, do crossword puzzles, knit, telephone their stockbrokers or bookies, or take a nap.

This interval on the sound stage may afford you some free time, but don't count on it. You may snatch a few minutes to grab a cup of coffee and the ubiquitous doughnut, or dash out to the washroom—something you cannot do while shooting is in progress, no matter how urgently nature calls.

(When asked what is an essential prerequisite for a continuity supervisor, I reply, "A strong bladder.") I also recommend that you keep a raincoat, overshoes, and umbrella handy for rainy days. The washrooms on a studio lot are always a distance from the sound stages, and for good reason: the flushing of toilets comes through the sound system like the roar of a wounded buffalo, with disastrous results for the scene in progress. (A word of advice: It is imperative that you inform the first or second assistant director that you are leaving the stage. The reason is that they can cover for you if an emergency arises.)

The possibility that you will indulge in any of the aforementioned pastimes is remote. In all probability, you will be asked by some member of the crew for information as to who is in the next shot, what's the time element, or details of wardrobe, makeup, props, or set dressing. Or perhaps a member of the executive staff will want to know something: what time did they start lighting, how many setups are planned, how many pages in this sequence, how long will the scene run? Your responses to all the questions must be quick and accurate. And there are other duties you will attend to while the stage is being prepared.

Script Revisions

If revised pages have been distributed, you will use this time period to adjust your script. It is essential that you keep your script pages up to the minute. There will be times when yours will be the only script that is current and complete.

Cuing Actors

During the waiting period, an actor may ask you to *cue* lines. That's another facet of your craft. Cuing lines means prompting the dialogue while the actors study and memorize their speeches. Actors refer to their pages of script as *sides*. For a three-page scene, an actor will say, "I've got three sides in this scene." You may often have to go wherever the actors happen to be—in dressing rooms, at makeup tables, or anywhere on the sound stage.

There is a basic method for cuing: you speak the last sentence (or last few words) of the speech that leads into the rehearsing actor's next speech. (For more information on the subject, see "The Pick-up Shot" in Chapter 5, and the section on "Covering Close-ups" in Chapter 10.)

You may be called upon to *run lines* with a group of actors who wish to rehearse their scene ensemble. Rehearsing in this manner entails a slightly different cuing approach: you follow the dialogue as each actor recites his or her lines, and when one of the actors falters, you prompt (cue) that particular speech.

Scene Reading

Sometimes the director wishes to have a scene reading. For this, the performers convene with the director in a quiet corner or in one of the dressing rooms. The actors recite the dialogue and the director discusses the fine points of motivation and interpretation. At these sessions you will make note of any suggested changes, either in dialogue or business/action. Your notations may be vitally important at the next rehearsal.

As you can see, your status is anything but static. With experience, you will learn to assess your priorities for these extracurricular diversions and use the time to your best advantage.

CAMERA REHEARSAL
WITH PRINCIPALS

As the technical crews near the finish of their work, the DP signals the first assistant director that the stage is now ready for the *first team* (the principal actors). And the first assistant director instructs the second assistant director to once again summon the actors to the stage.

Having carefully watched all the operations taking shape on the stage, and before the cast arrives, the first assistant director inquires of the director whether any foreseeable contingencies need to be considered before the camera rehearsal. If all is well, the first assistant director calls out, "Let's have a bell." The sound mixer strikes a bell or buzzer. This is the signal for everyone on the sound stage (or set location) to refrain from chattering, moving around, or making any noise. "Quiet!" yells the first assistant, then addresses the actors with, "Places, everyone, please." The stand-ins now leave the set, and the actors move into their starting places in the scene. This will be a *dry-camera rehearsal* (no film turning).

At this early point in rehearsals, it is advisable to make only light pencil markings of the actors' movements; these may have to be erased quickly. But when the scene is actually being filmed, you will make bolder notations so you can spot them easily when the scene is being covered (more on this in Chapters 10 and 11). You will invariably find that when the camera is rolling with the performance, the actors' actions do not fall on precisely the same words as they did in rehearsals. Remember: only the action and dialogue that appear on film are your concern for *matching*. But more on this later.

For this rehearsal, the actors may be partially dressed in their stage wardrobe. While the actors make their way into the set, you will have an opportunity to quickly sketch in some wardrobe notes. Keep in mind, however, that actors do not always get into full proper attire until the last *dress rehearsal*. If you wish, you may ask the costumers what the actual wardrobe will be. But be cautioned: your notes must reflect the exact wardrobe that is in the film—not the costumers' records. It bears repeating: Only what is put on film matters to you for matching purposes. As mentioned earlier, the wardrobe notes you keep are solely for your purposes. Wardrobe accuracy is the responsibility of the wardrobe department; your responsibility rests with the state of the articles of clothing being handled during the performance, and matching their conditions from shot to shot.

When making wardrobe notes, write descriptive details: gray felt hat, brim down; black knit tie; maroon/blue diagonal-stripe tie; pink polka-dot blouse over khaki pants; brown cardigan over short-sleeved white shirt tucked inside blue jeans; yellow T-neck sweater over green/gold plaid skirt; floral shirt over beige pants. Abbreviate as much as possible. Small hieroglyphics instead of wordy descriptions can be timesaving and often make spotting mistakes easier.

In the first dry-camera rehearsal, the actors go through their roles with more refinement, so the camera operator, viewing the action through the camera lens, can make sure that the composition of each move is framed precisely and in perfect focus, and that the boom mike following the actors does not dip into the picture frame or cast a shadow in the set.

The dolly grip—the person who wields the moving camera—also watches the rehearsal carefully to become familiar with the action. At times the dolly grip will ask you on which word of dialogue an actor will make a move; the dolly grip must anticipate this action in order to instantly push the camera to its next position. From your script notes, you should be able to respond without hesitation.

The actors *run through* a scene several times, each time more fluently, more expressively, more emotionally. The director watches for dramatic excellence, the DP watches for lighting excellence, and the camera operator watches for perfect framing and focus. The scene is rehearsed as many times as is necessary until the performance is flawless—ready to be committed to film.

During rehearsals, your eyes must closely follow the dialogue. Most important, watch for ad libs and altered phrasing. When this occurs, ask the director for approval of the substitution. If the director disapproves, the actor must be corrected immediately. The director will do this or instruct you to do so. Sometimes an altered phrase that omits the proper word-cue will cause dismay to the other actor, or it may spoil the rhythmic pattern of the dialogue (this is especially true in comedy).

It is vitally important that you know your script backwards and forwards, so you can instantly recognize an inadvertently changed word or phrase that conflicts with a previous or subsequent scene. The change must be brought to the director's attention without delay—not after the actor has committed the incorrect words to memory or, worse, to film. Be on the alert for inaccuracies in the mention of a date, an address, an amount of money, or the time on a clock. If the director opts to keep the deviation, you will have to change the affected unshot scenes to make them compatible. But if the change conflicts with a scene that has already been shot, the dialogue in the immediate scene must remain as written. Be on the alert, also, for the proper pronunciation of names and technical terms. It is your responsibility to catch and correct every variation that occurs during repeated rehearsals—and to do so prior to shooting. If a conflicting ad lib or a mispronounced word happens during the filming of a scene, it will be necessary to redo the shot and correct the mistake.

During run-throughs an actor may whisper, "I'm up," or "Line, please." Those words are for your ears. The actor has forgotten the next speech, or part of it, and it's up to you to *throw the line*. During all rehearsals, you should closely follow the dialogue on the page so you can prompt the needed line without missing a beat.

Also, while watching rehearsals, be on the alert for body positions, overt actions, and dialogue. Those details may be critical for matching in subsequent coverage. Jot down a key word or a symbol at the appropriate spot on the page. With experience, this skill will become second nature. NOTE: You may throw a line during rehearsals but NEVER while the camera is rolling. The adage that every rule has an exception applies here. The exception to this rule will be discussed in Chapter 5 under "The Pick-up Shot."

TIMING REHEARSALS

At the first really refined rehearsal of the master scene, you should attempt to get an overall timing of the performance. If fluffs in dialogue or action, or technical malfunctions, cause stops and starts during this rehearsal, be sure to click off your stopwatch at the break points and be ready to instantly click it on again at the precise word or action that continues the scene. Thus you will get an approximate running time of the shot.

A good habit is to time every rehearsal until and including the dress rehearsal. By comparing each timing, you will learn whether the pace of the scene is being accelerated or slowed down in the playing. The practice of constantly operating your stopwatch during all rehearsals will make you adept at clocking the crucial timing of a performance while the camera is rolling. The technique of timing shots to get actual picture-running time is discussed under "Timing the Performance" in Chapter 5.

With diligence and experience, you will eventually acquire the facility to automatically handle the stopwatch while simultaneously writing, seeing, hearing, and speaking. It becomes simple routine.

DRESS REHEARSAL

After several rehearsals, and after all the creative and technical components of the scene have been fine-tuned, the director will declare, "Let's have a dress rehearsal." That calls for a final, disciplined run-through with proper tempo, dramatic fervor, proper wardrobe, functioning props, and camera moves, exactly as if the scene were being filmed. But there will be one distracting detail: the tissues tucked into the collars of the performers to prevent the makeup from soiling their garments. These tissues will be removed in good time.

NUMBER THE SPEECHES

When the dress rehearsal is pretty well locked in (almost ready for the camera), you may choose to add another detail on your script page; that is, to consecutively number each speech within the scene. This could prove helpful during shooting. The purpose is explained in Chapter 7.

SHOT DESCRIPTION*

Between rehearsals, you will have opportunity to write the *shot description* of the scene about to be filmed. This is a vital detail in your continuity script. It is your communication to the film editor of what is being put on film. The description is a concise summary of the action of the scene and the camera moves. This legend is written on the blank left-hand page opposite the scene page of the script. Following is a sample shot description:

> Start MS angle toward office door. Smith enters. Pan his walk X-L-R to doorway into Charles office. Hold Full 4/Sh over Smith L-Shld to 3 seated at desk: Charles, Mary, Bert—dial.—As Smith moves to f.g. desk. DI to Tite/4: Smith (stg), Charles, Mary, Bert—dial.—Mary rises and exits shot R-L. Smith follows. DI to Tite/2: Charles & Bert—dial.—Charles rises and exits shot R-L.—ZI to CU Bert. He rises, picks up phone, dials, and talks.

When writing shot descriptions, develop the habit of writing the names of characters in the positions they hold (standing or sitting) as seen in the camera. Train yourself to see persons and objects in their respective positions in the frame. For example, in the master (full shot) Charles is on camera left (CL) seated right of Mary, and Mary is on camera right (CR) seated left of Charles. In writing the shot description of their closer two shot, do not write 2/Sh: Mary and Charles. Name them as they appeared in the master: Charles and Mary. In that way, you will never make the mistake of placing characters in incorrect positions during coverage.

---

*See Appendix A for a comprehensive list of abbreviations used in shot descriptions.

5

Getting the Scene on Film

THE SLATING PROCESS

The assigning of slate and take numbers is the unequivocal jurisdiction of the continuity supervisor, since you "hold" the script during shooting. When you announce the appropriate numbers, the slate operator chalks them onto the slate, and the sound mixer speaks the numbers into the recording panel.

The Slate

The *slate*, sometimes called the *clapboard* or the *sticks*, is an industry tool devised to identify every shot made for the editor and the laboratory. The mechanism of the slate synchronizes the visual with the audio. The two elements function in unison, but separately. The action of the scene is recorded on film while the dialogue and sounds inherent in the scene are recorded on tape. In editing, the two conventions are combined. When picture and sound are not in sync, the actors' lip formations do not fit the sounds of their words.

The slate is a square piece of wood, painted black. Attached to the top are two hinged bars with black and white diagonal stripes. At a fixed moment, the two bars are snapped together to make the sound of a CLAP. (The slate operator is sometimes referred to as the *Clapper*.)

The camera second assistant—who functions also as the slate operator—prepares the slate in advance. (See Figure 5.1.)

Figure 5.1

The Take

Takes are made in conjunction with each slate number. A take refers to the attempt to make a shot—that is, to record a scene onto the camera and sound track. Takes are repeated as many times as necessary until the director is satisfied with the result.

The takes are numbered sequentially, and with every change of scene number on the slate, the corresponding takes always begin with number 1.

When a take is satisfactory, the director orders it to be printed (processed at the laboratory). After every *printed take,* a new slate number is routinely assigned. However, this rule does not apply when the director requests an additional take of a shot that had been previously okayed for printing. In that case, you will announce the next consecutive take number. Further explanation appears later in this chapter, under "Multiple Prints."

SYSTEMS OF SLATING

There are two commonly used systems of slating:

1. Scene-Number Slating

Slating by scene numbers is the most direct method. Every slate number represents a script scene number or an *auxiliary scene number* that has been created by the continuity supervisor in the course of shooting (more on this in Chapter 6).

2. Consecutive-Number Slating

Slating by consecutive numbers (also referred to as *numerical slate numbering*) is an optional method, albeit a widely used one. Ask your editors which system they prefer. With consecutive-number slating, you will announce "Slate number one" on the first day of shooting (regardless of where the scene occurs in the script) and continue with the next consecutive number for every slate change. Slate number 1 may apply to Scene 96 and slate number 2 may apply to Scene 5.

Consecutive-number slating mandates some additional clerical work. It is imperative that you record, alongside the slate number, the number of the corresponding script scene that is being filmed. This detail of recording the scene number alongside the consecutive slate number must be meticulously followed through in your script notes, in the Daily Continuity Log, and especially in the Daily Editor's Log; otherwise it will be impossible for the editor to put the pieces of film together in proper sequence.

YOUR PLACE AT THE CAMERA

Always position yourself as close to the camera's viewpoint as possible, even if you have to crouch on the floor or stand on a ladder. It is imperative that you observe the scene from the camera's angle, not from the periphery of the scene. Your immediate concern is the image that is in the camera frame at any given angle, whether the camera is stationary or moving. Therefore, you must choose the best vantage point from which to see and hear every nuance of action and dialogue during the filming. It's a demerit if you have to confess that you did not hear a word or see a particular detail in the performance because you were not positioned in the right place.

You may even have to ask someone (perhaps even the executive producer)—diplomatically—to move to another spot so that he or she is not standing in front of you and blocking your vision. By the same token, you should not, in your zeal to get the best station, block the director's vision.

When a set is lit for filming, the rest of the stage is in darkness. So try to

68

find a spot where you can steal some light from the set. But always be sure to sit or stand out of the range of an actor's eyeline. Your constant hand movements and turning of pages may distract the actor's concentration. Some performers become unnerved by this intrusion.

If you have to stand on a ladder to observe the scene properly, ask the gaffer to install a work light for you (see Figure 5.2).

READY TO ROLL

At the completion of a thorough dress rehearsal, the director may announce, "We're ready to roll," or "Ready to shoot" (the two expressions are interchangeable). The announcement is a signal to all concerned personnel to get to their posts. The actors remain in the set, and the first assistant director calls in the *wrecking crew*—an affectionate term for the makeup, hairdressing, and wardrobe people, who will enter the set to give their last-minute finishing touches to the actors. But first the DP calls, "Kill the lights," and the gaffer switches off all the huge technical lamps. (These lights generate excessive heat and consume enormous amounts of electricity.) Now the hairdresser smooths a lock of hair; the costumer adjusts a wrinkle in a garment; the makeup artist mops up the actors' perspiration, retouches their makeup, and, finally, removes the tissue from the actors' collars.

At the same time, the camera assistant picks up the tapes or wooden chips that marked stage positions on the floor for the actors. As the crew leaves the set, the assistant director calls, "Places, please." That's the cue for the performers to take their respective starting positions in the scene, or the places from which they will make entrances onto the set. And now the gaffer switches on all the lights that work in the set.

FIRST SHOT OF THE DAY

When every detail is in place and everybody is in readiness:

The AD shouts ...."Let's have a bell."
The Mixer signals....................................ONE BELL or BUZZ
(This also activates the red light
  outside the stage door, which
  warns that no one must enter or
  exit the door during shooting.)
A hush falls on the stage and the
  magic of moviemaking begins:
The Continuity Supervisor
  announces ...."Scene 26, Take One."
The Camera Second Assistant (Slate
  Operator) chalks the numbers on
  the slate and repeats ...."Scene 26, Take One."

Figure 5.2

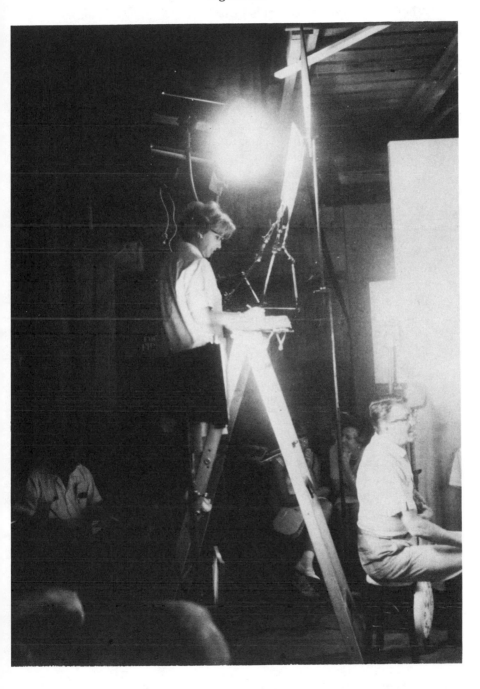

The AD yells	"Quiet!"
When silence falls on the stage, the AD calls	"Roll 'em" or "Roll camera."
The Camera Operator, peering through the lens and certain that the picture is in perfect frame and focus, snaps the camera switch on	CLICK
The Mixer voices the slate number into the recorder	"Scene 26, Take One."
There is silence for a few beats, until the recording rate of speed coincides with the camera's rate of speed.	
The Mixer calls out	"Speed."
The Slate Operator holds the slate up to camera's view.	
The Camera Operator, seeing the slate in the frame, announces	"Rolling."
After a beat	"Mark it."
The Slate Operator (who at this juncture gets the title Clapper) snaps the two striped bars (*clapsticks*) together	CLAP
(This sound signals the editor that film and sound track are in perfect sync.) The Slate Operator then dashes out of the set.	
The Director, after a beat, calls	"Action."
Now the stage becomes alive with the actors giving their best performances. And the scene is transformed into the motion picture we see in the theater or on television.	
At the completion of each take, or if something goes wrong with the take:	
The Director calls	"Cut."
The Mixer signals	TWO BELLS or BUZZES
(This signal also switches off the red door-light, announcing that normal activity may resume.)	

NOTE: With every change of slate or take number, the entire litany is repeated: the AD calls, "Let's have a bell," one bell SOUNDS, the director calls "Action" and "Cut," and the two bells or buzzers SOUND.

A new slate number is mandated:

☐ Every time the camera is repositioned (even slightly).

☐ Every time the camera lens is changed, even when the camera remains in the same position.

☐ Every time there is a *pick-up shot* (see page 74).

Every slate number constitutes a *setup*—except in the case of pick-ups. There is a correlation between the record of slate numbers and the total number of setups recorded for the day's shoot (see "Setup Count" under "Daily Progress Report" in Chapter 7).

END SLATES

When the slate operator holds up the slate at the start of a shot (the *head slate*), you should always look to see that all the information on it is correct. If you notice any error, alert the slate operator to be prepared to *end slate* (sometimes called *end marker* or *tail slate*). Immediately upon completion of the shot, and before both the camera operator and sound mixer switch off, the slate operator will shout "End slate" and hold up the corrected slate—in upside-down position—to be photographed. But if the camera is switched off prematurely, there will be no end slate on that piece of film, and the editor will not be apprised of the incorrect head slate. It will then be incumbent upon you to notify the editor that the head slate is inaccurate. It is important to note "E/S" (for end slate) at the slate number in your script notes and on the Daily Editor's Log.

End slates are also used when the harsh sound of the clapper is impractical at the start of a shot. This rule also applies when making shots of sleeping babies or animals that would be disturbed. Under those circumstances, a silent hand motion (instead of the slate) at the head of the shot signals the editor that there is an upside-down slate at the tail end of the shot.

CAMERA ROLLING*

When you hear "Action," snap your stopwatch on and concentrate on the performance. If there is a great deal of activity in the scene, don't attempt to make notes on everyone and everything there. From the rehearsals, you have gotten a good overall picture of what is taking place in the scene, now *keep your eyes on the principal actors* (the slogan is "Stay with the money").

---

* A little aside about stopwatches. Many available today are noiseless. But in earlier years, when one pressed the knob to activate the watch, the click was picked up on the soundtrack like a clap of thunder. In those days, I would hold the watch under my arm or between my knees everytime it had to be started or stopped. If you do not use a digital timepiece, be aware of the click that your stopwatch makes.

Copious Notes

With practice and experience, you will become adept at writing hastily while seeing and hearing everything that is taking place in the set. And sometimes you will achieve all this while sitting or standing where there is insufficient light. You will discover that you can mentally retain a host of details. But there is good reason for profuse jottings on the script page while a performance is in progress. It is fine to rely on your photographic memory if you are endowed with one, but something written is less disputable—provided, of course, that the notation is accurate.

Back Matching during Filming

The procedure for back matching during filming is not unlike back matching when breaking down the script. Here, while shooting is in progress, you will notate carryover details in preceding and subsequent scenes. For example, Scene 44 is being filmed before Scene 42. In Scene 42 a fight takes place, during which the actor is hit and sustains a black eye. The writer, of course, does not specify which eye. However, in preparing for Scene 44, the makeup artist arbitrarily blackened the actor's right eye. Consequently, you will make a notation at Scene 44: "right eye blackened." Then as soon as time permits, you should turn the script pages to Scene 42 and make a conspicuous note: "Injury to right eye."

If, while shooting Scene 44, you neglected to make the necessary notation at Scene 42—and if your memory did not serve you—something contrary may happen while shooting Scene 42: the exchange of fisticuffs might end up with the actor holding his hand over his left eye, the punch having landed on the wrong eye. It is your responsibility, when going into rehearsal for Scene 42, to inform the actor (or stuntperson) who does the socking that he or she must aim at the opponent's right eye—because it has to match Scene 44, which is already on film.

Sometimes, even with the most conscientious prior instructions, errors do occur in the frenzy of staging a fight. Should that happen, a portion of the scene, or all of it, may have to be done over in order to match the previously shot scene.

Let us take another example. When shooting Scene 3, a chair is broken in a scuffle. There is a time lapse between Scene 3 and Scene 6, but storywise, there is no way that someone could have replaced or removed the broken chair. Consequently, that broken chair must be in its place at the start of shooting Scene 6. Once again, while shooting Scene 3, you must turn to Scene 6 and make notation that the broken chair must be in view to match Scene 3. The filming of Scene 6 may not take place until weeks later. While this detail is essentially the property department's responsibility, your double-check could prevent a mismatch.

"Cut . . . Print"

When the director is pleased with the performance and the technical departments do not announce any problems at the finish of a shot, the director calls "Cut . . . Print." Hearing this, you will draw a circle around that take number; the slate operator and mixer will do likewise on their respective logs. This piece of film will be printed at the laboratory.

Camera's records, sound's records, and your Daily Continuity Log must be in absolute accord for each and every slate and take number. Make a point of *checking prints* with the slate operator and the sound mixer several times during the day. Should a discrepancy show up on any of the logs, it must be corrected before the camera and sound reports are transferred to the laboratory or the editor.

No Print

If "no print" is declared after a completed take, it means the director was dissatisfied with the result and wishes to have the shot repeated. You will announce the next take number on the same slate and continue with consecutive numbers until the shot is accepted for printing. Always ask the director the reason for rejecting the take and note the reason alongside the take number. This important reference notation will be explained later in this chapter, under "Out Takes."

Who Calls "Cut"?

Only three people may call "Cut" to stop the rolling of the camera.

1. The director—when dissatisfied with the performance.
2. The camera operator—when the camera goes awry because of mechanical difficulty, such as film buckling, battery failure, or light shift; when the framing is off because the actors have not "hit their marks" as established in rehearsal; when the boom mike or its shadow has crept into the picture.
3. The mixer—when there is a technical sound problem, an off-screen disturbance (e.g., overhead airplane, loud coughing), or when the actor's dialogue is indistinguishable.

The continuity supervisor *never* cuts the shot—not even when the actors have spoken incorrect dialogue or made incorrect gestures. After the call "Cut," you will apprise the director of the flaws you noted.

The director may choose to do the shot over from the beginning (the expression is *from the top*), or the decision may be to repeat only the faulty portion. If the shot is to be repeated from the top, you will announce the *next take number* on the same slate number. The performance will be repeated until the director calls "Cut . . . Print."

The Pick-up Shot

If only the faulty portion of the scene is to be reshot, the director will call for a *pick-up shot.* In that case, you will announce a *new slate number* and start with Take One, as opposed to simply using another take number when reshooting from the top of the scene.

Pick-up shots are usually designated by appending a letter (A, B, C, etc.) to the original slate number. However, when the slating system is based on consecutive numbers, the next consecutive number will necessarily be the pick-up number as well. Therefore, it is important that you add PU (for pick-up) alongside that number. This notation should also appear alongside the number on your lined script page (delineated in Chapter 7), as well as on the Daily Continuity Log and the Daily Editor's Log (see Chapter 6, Figures 6.1 and 6.2).

There are several ways in which a pick-up shot is recorded:

1. By reslating. A new slate number is the simplest method for both you and the editor.
2. By not reslating and doing the pick-up with the camera rolling. This entails a different approach for different circumstances:
   a. *False Start.* If a fluff in dialogue or action occurs near the beginning of the shot, the director will—while the camera continues to roll—prompt the actors to "start from the top." That means going back to the beginning of the shot, repeating the action and dialogue, and continuing the performance to the end. When this irregularity occurs, be sure to make the notation FS (for false start) alongside the take number. It is necessary that you also note FS alongside the slate number on the Daily Editor's Log. After viewing the film on the Moviola (projection machine), the editor will then cut off the defective front piece of the shot and carefully synchronize the good start with the corresponding sound track.

   Be sure to reset your stopwatch at the second start of the shot for accurate timing of the scene.
   b. *Throw a Line.* When a fluff occurs in the middle or toward the end of the shot, the director may opt not to cut the shot. Instead, with the camera rolling, the director will prompt the actors to go back to an earlier speech or business, correct the fluff, and then continue to the end of the scene.

   At this juncture, let us recall the rule mentioned in Chapter 4—"Never throw a line while the camera is rolling." Here is the exception to that rule. You *will* throw the line while the camera is rolling. Your eyes must quickly spot the exact dialogue on the page so you can instantly cue the actor with the earlier speech indicated by the director.

When prompting (cuing) dialogue, you must always start at the *top of a speech*. The reason for this rule is technical. The editor cannot *cut in* on an actor's face during the middle of his or her speech. Mark the precise points on the page where the pick-up clearly begins and ends, and make a notation to the editor about the disruption in the shot.

THE BRIDGE SHOT

When a piece of flawed film remains in a shot—picked up without reslating, as described above—that faulty portion of film must be excised, and a suitable piece of film must be inserted as a *bridge shot*. The bridge shot is necessary in order to achieve a smooth transition of the action cut in the master shot. In editing, the term that denotes the *joining* of pieces of cut film is called *splicing*.

A bridge shot may be in the form of:

1. A separate close-up of one of the characters in the scene.
2. An appropriate angle change for that portion of the scene in which the action or dialogue was disrupted.
3. An effective shot of some other subject matter, called a *cutaway*. (Another aspect of the cutaway shot is delineated under "Covering Wrong Action" in Chapter 10.)

It is essential to provide the editor with a bridge shot for every pick-up made, whether the master shot was reslated at the break or the correction made with the camera rolling.

MULTIPLE PRINTS

At times, when the director has okayed a take for printing and then opted to shoot one more of the same, one slate number will include more than one printed take. In such instances, you will announce the next consecutive take number on the same slate and continue with successive take numbers until another one is designated for printing. Always ask the director the reason for the repeat and note it alongside the take number. Sometimes the director simply wants to see if a better performance will emerge. If the second printed take varies in any way from the first one, make a note to the editor of the dissimilarity in the two shots. The decision as to which print will appear in the finished film is made in the editing room.

On occasion, the director will instruct you to print one or more of the incomplete takes. Be sure to circle the numbers of these takes and pass the information on to the slate operator and the mixer so that their daily reports and yours will be in absolute accord.

ALTERNATIVE SHOTS

When a master shot has been printed and the director shoots the scene again from another camera viewpoint or for any substantive change in the performance, that piece of film constitutes an *alternative shot*. The print that will be used in the final cut of the picture is decided in the editing room.

Sometimes an alternative shot is made in anticipation of *film censorship*. One version of the scene may be acceptable in some areas (domestic or foreign) and prohibited in others.

In any case, you will assign a new slate number (in keeping with the slating system used) and make notation in your continuity script and the Daily Editor's Log as to how the two shots differ in action and/or dialogue.

OUT TAKES

Takes that are listed but not printed are called *out takes*. These may be complete or incomplete. It is good policy to clock the running time of every take. One reason is that in the event a flaw that was caused in the laboratory (scratch, fog) appears in a strip of film, the editor will immediately refer to your continuity script and search for out takes. Your notes on the timings of these takes and the reasons for not printing them will help the editor determine whether there is sufficient footage in those takes to overcome the predicament. With clever cutting, several out takes can be intercut with the good portions of the damaged film. Thus, the editor can salvage the original sequence and avert a costly retake.

Another reason for timing each take is for the occasion when the camera first assistant (who closely watches the camera film gauge) asks you if 120 feet of film is sufficient for the next take or if the camera needs to be reloaded. Based on your timings of the recorded takes, you can give the answer without hesitation.

Much depends on your quick and accurate answer: (a) By avoiding the camera reload, the mood of the scene is preserved, and time on the set is saved. (b) By utilizing the film remaining in the camera, the waste of *short ends* of raw stock is diminished. This can be cost-effective for a small production company. The most distressing and costly mistake is to start a shot and run out of film. By recording the timing of every take, you will have confidence in stating whether or not the shot can be made with the amount of film in the magazine (see "Conversion Table" and "Conversion Chart" in Appendix B).

RETAKES

When it is necessary to redo a shot that has already been printed at the laboratory, the new shot is called a *retake*. To slate a retake, use the slate number of the original shot and precede it with an R (for retake). This applies to both scene-number and consecutive-number slating. With a consecutive-numbered slate, be sure to note the scene number that corresponds to the original (consecutive) slate number.

MULTIPLE CAMERAS*

When shooting with more than one camera, a prominent letter is attached to the outside of each camera, identifying it as A-camera, B-camera, C-camera, and so on. The slates, likewise, carry the corresponding letters A, B, C. After each take, the slates are photographed separately for each camera.

It is necessary to write a separate description of the shot that each camera is holding. Also, note the lens sizes and each camera's directional moves, if any.

A helpful hint: Note on which side of A-camera the other cameras are positioned. This will preclude any controversy regarding directions or progression when making subsequent shots in that sequence. Often, in staging a scene, a character may walk out of the range of B-camera into the range of A-camera, or vice versa. To be sure of accurate screen direction, I draw a diagram of a three-walled set with configurations that denote the camera position. The diagram is placed either on the left-hand page with the shot description, or in the right-hand margin of the script page, per the figure on page 53.

The Common Slate

At times, if the cameras are in proximity to each other, only one slate (called the *common slate*) is photographed to accommodate two or more cameras. This is a timesaving measure.

TIMING THE PERFORMANCE

Starting your stopwatch as the director calls "Action" and clicking it off at the sound of "Cut . . . Print" will give you the running time of the shot, but not of the picture. *Picture-running time* is not based on the amount of footage printed, but on the amount of usable film—the portion of the footage that maintains the continuity and dramatic essence of every shot.

A workable approach is to first get a fairly accurate timing of the master shot. But that may not always be the final timing of the scene. Other considerations intrude, such as an actor taking a few seconds at the start of the scene to "work up to the action." You must quickly reckon how many seconds to deduct from your stopwatch time. Inasmuch as some twenty or

---

* It is advisable to include in your deal memo that you will receive additional pay when multiple cameras are used.

more master shots are made in a day's shoot, you can appreciate how much useless film will be left on the cutting-room floor, and how inaccurate your calculation of picture-running time would be if you did not make adjustments to determine the final timing of each scene for your daily report.

Another adjustment to master-shot timing occurs when filming *coverage shots* (see Chapter 10). Actors will sometimes *linger* on their close-up shots. Your timing expertise will dictate how many seconds need to be added to the total for the master shot. Several prolonged close-ups can significantly stretch the picture time. Also, a piece of business (for example, comedy action) may run longer or shorter in the closer angle than in the master shot. So it becomes necessary to frequently adjust the recorded picture time for the master shot.

Another important factor that influences your timing of a show is your ability to discern what is excessive in the shot, such as long walks to doors and exits, pregnant pauses, or drawn-out histrionics.

The timing of a film carries substantial responsibility. When your daily reports indicate that the filming is going beyond the projected length of the show (*running long*), the director and the producer may be inclined to make deletions in the script. But if your timings are not accurate, the film may end up too short. Conversely, if your daily reports indicate that there is less film than needed for the projected length of the show (*running short*), the director and the producer may add or lengthen scenes. In that case, if your timings are inaccurate, the finished film may end up too long. In both these circumstances—assuming that no script changes were made—the editor will have to spend tedious hours trying to either expand or contract the film footage to acceptable length. This is very costly to the company.

If you possess an innate sense of dramaturgy, you can be instrumental in avoiding drastic measures. The pacing of scenes—from a directorial standpoint—may be the reason why a film is running long or short. In the case of running too long, you might suggest to the director that the playing time of some of the scenes be accelerated in order to eliminate the need to delete or shorten script scenes. In the case of running too short, you might suggest to the director that the playing time of some of the scenes be prolonged in order to avoid the expense of unnecessarily writing and filming added scenes.

Assuming that your timing is consistently accurate, you can use the following rule of thumb: if your timing at the halfway point in the script reflects practically two-thirds of the scheduled time for the show, then the shoot is obviously running *long*. On the other hand, if your timing at the halfway point in the script reflects only a third of the scheduled show time, then the shoot is running *short*. At that point, it is advisable to discuss the picture time with the director or the producer or both. It is within their province to resolve the predicament.

A helpful hint: when you feel uncertain about your timing, have a conference with the editor. After viewing all the dailies, the editor can make an educated guess as to whether or not your timing of the film will be on target, and you can adjust accordingly. The editor can manipulate the picture time to some degree. Scenes can be shortened by trimming the fronts and ends of master shots (where possible) and by judiciously clipping drawn-out close-ups. Inversely, the picture time can be lengthened by using every inch of the master shots (within reason) and holding longer on the close-ups when feasible. Naturally, these modifications have to be accomplished without detracting from the impact of the performance or the ambience of the scene. In the final analysis, it is your timing expertise upon which the company depends.

It is good practice to keep a progressive total of picture time in your Daily Continuity Log. In that way, you will always have up-to-the-minute picture time at your fingertips. This is the information the producer is most likely to ask for at any given hour of the day. Only you have the answer. And if you can reply with alacrity—without doing arithmetic while the producer is breathing down your neck—your efficiency will not go unrecognized.

Timing Traveling Shots

When the script specifies TRAVELING SHOT, the scene will be filmed and the dialogue recorded while actors are riding in a vehicle.

One method of shooting traveling scenes is from another traveling vehicle, called an *insert car*. This vehicle houses all the camera and sound equipment, with space for the technical personnel. The insert car travels from a vantage point on the road, with the camera focused on the principal vehicle and the actors inside. (The second vehicle is not always a professional insert car. The equipment and crew may be accommodated in a sedan, a convertible, or a pickup truck.)

A second method of filming a traveling shot is with a camera operator strapped to the outside of the actors' vehicle and focusing a hand-held camera. The sound mixer, with tape recorder, is hidden inside the vehicle, crouching on the floor of the car. The director, equipped with earphones, crouches alongside. If there is room in the vehicle, you too squeeze in with the others. In this cramped position, with earphones clamped to your ears, holding your script, pencil, and stopwatch, you will follow the dialogue while timing the shot.

A third method is to strategically mount a prefocused camera on the body of the traveling vehicle. Since there will be no camera technician to operate the camera, the actor in the car will activate the camera by clapping his or her hands at the start of the shot; another clap at the end of the shot will signal the camera shutoff. In this operation, the same personnel mentioned above will be in the back of the vehicle.

If there is no room for you in the vehicle, your alternative for knowing what has been put on film is to meet with the sound mixer after the take and have the tape recorder played back. With script and stopwatch in hand, you will time the shot and listen to the dialogue, noting any deviations from the script. Words or improvised lines that vary from the script should be brought to the director's attention immediately for an okay or decision to make a pick-up.

Timing Runby Shots

Shooting a traveling vehicle with a stationary camera and no sound track is referred to as a *runby*. Your timing of these shots will be based on your educated guess at how much film will be dramatic picture time, irrespective of the amount of footage used (eighty feet of film may end up as six seconds on the screen).

Timing Telephone Conversations

Telephone conversations are not filmed simultaneously. Each character's dialogue is filmed at a different time. You will clock only the speeches of the character on-camera. During filming, the responding dialogue is delivered by someone other than the cast actor (because the actor for that half of the conversation is not yet on salary). The procedure is as follows: you snap on your stopwatch at the start of the speech of the actor on-camera, and shut it off at the end of the speech. Your stopwatch is disengaged while the off-camera person speaks. At the finish of the off-camera speech, you start the watch again and repeat the procedure for each succeeding on-camera speech. This gives you the picture time for half of the telephone conversation. At a later date, when the responding actor is on-camera, you will follow the same procedure; that will give you the picture time for the second half of the telephone conversation. You will record in your Daily Continuity Log the timing of each side of the conversation on the date it is filmed.

Timing Fast and Slow Motion*

A critical adjustment in picture time must be made when filming is done in fast motion or slow motion.

Fast motion is achieved with an *undercranked* camera. This means that the camera is running at a speed lower than its standard speed of 24 frames per second (fps) while the subjects perform at their normal pace. When this film is put through the Moviola (projection machine), which is fixed at 24 fps, the subjects' movements appear speeded up on the screen. The formula for calculating accurate timing of shots in fast motion is as follows: *multiply* your stopwatch time by the adjusted camera speed and *divide* by the standard camera-running speed.

---

* All fast- and slow-motion shooting is done without sound (MOS) because sound equipment, like the projection equipment, is not geared for variable speeds, as is the camera.

Let us say your stopwatch registers 21 seconds for a shot made at 16 fps:

$$
\begin{array}{rl}
21 & \text{seconds stopwatch time} \\
\times\ 16 & \text{fps camera speed} \\
\hline
336 & \text{feet camera-running footage}
\end{array}
$$

336 divided by 24 fps (standard camera speed) equals 14 seconds of picture time (as against 21 seconds clocked on the stopwatch).

You will record 14 seconds as picture-running time.

Slow motion is achieved with an *overcranked* camera. This means that the camera is running at a speed higher than its standard 24 fps while the subjects perform at their normal pace. When this film is put through the Moviola, which is fixed at 24 fps, the subjects' movements appear slowed down on the screen. The formula for calculating accurate timing of shots in slow motion is as follows: *multiply* your stopwatch time by the adjusted camera speed and *divide* by the standard camera-running speed.

Let us say your stopwatch registers 21 seconds for a shot made at 36 fps:

$$
\begin{array}{rl}
21 & \text{seconds stopwatch time} \\
\times\ 36 & \text{fps camera speed} \\
\hline
756 & \text{feet camera-running footage}
\end{array}
$$

756 divided by 24 fps (standard camera speed) equals 31½ seconds (as against 21 seconds clocked on the stopwatch).

You will record 31 1/2 seconds as picture-running time.

Time/Footage Conversion

Footage is the measurement that relates to the number of feet of exposed film, as registered on the camera's footage counter. A 35mm magazine holds approximately 1,000 feet of raw stock, and the film runs through the camera at the rate of 90 feet per minute.

Should you forget to snap your stopwatch on when the camera starts to roll, don't panic. Immediately after the take, ask the camera first assistant (focus puller) for the footage of that shot; then convert the footage to minutes and seconds for your records (see Appendix B for Conversion Table and Conversion Chart).

READING OFF-CAMERA DIALOGUE

On several occasions you may be called upon to read off-camera dialogue (sometimes the responding actor in a scene is not available, having been dismissed earlier to save company overtime). So there you are, delivering lines (with feeling)—and simultaneously watching the on-camera actors' movements, listening to their dialogue, making notations of any deviations from the script, and timing the take.

6

Recording the Day's Shoot

KEEPING TRACK OF DAILY DATA

By this time you are probably wondering how one keeps track of the myriad details that accumulate for the continuity supervisor in the course of a day's shoot. Let me assure you that if you do the job right, everything falls nicely into place.

The Daily Continuity Log (Figure 6.1) is your personal control sheet—your bible, so to speak. This record is a chronicle of the day's activity from start to finish and should be at your fingertips at all times. In the captioned columns, you will make systematic entries of:

☐ Every setup by slate number. When multiple cameras roll simultaneously, each camera is slated individually and recorded separately (e.g., Slate 71 [A-Camera] and Slate B-71 [B-Camera] are listed as two setups).

☐ All the respective printed takes of each slate number.

☐ The picture-time credit of all the master shots. (Remember: the picture time of master shots may have to be adjusted, as discussed under "Timing the Performance" in Chapter 5.)

☐ The page-count credit of all master shots.

NOTE: Do not list the time and page counts of the *coverage* shots. To do so would give you grossly inaccurate daily totals (more on this in Chapter 7 under "Daily Progress Report").

84

DAILY CONTINUITY LOG

PRODUCTION NO. 1560   DATE 8/20

TITLE _____   WORK DAY 4TH

Shoot. Call 7:30 A
1st Shot 8:04 A
Lunch 1:00 - 2:00 P
1st Shot 2:24 P
Dinner 7:00 - 7:30 P
1st Shot 7:45 P
Cam. Wrap 8:52 P
Snd Wrap 8:52 P

Scenes Covered
2 16 21 A42
3 17 41 7
4 18 42 8 PT
5 26 43
6 19 44 /17

Wild Tracks

Retakes

	Scenes	Pages
Total Script	60	36 7/8
Added	1	2/8
Deleted		
New Total	61	37 1/8
Shot Prior	23	17
Shot Today	17	7 7/8
To Date	40	24 7/8
To Do	21	12 2/8

* 84 MISSLATED 83 TK 2

ADD SC. A-42

CAM ROL	SND ROL	SET UP	SCENE	SLATE	PRNT	TIME	TOTL TIME	PAGES	TOTL PAGES
FORWARD		66	23				15:36		17
		1	2,3,4	71	4	.52	−	1−	
		2	3,4/6	B71	4	−	−		
		3	3,4/6	72	2	.06	.58		
		4	3,4/6	B72	1,2	−			
		5	4	73	1	−			
		6	5	74	2	.04	1.02	−1	1 1/8
		7	16-18	75	2	1.27	2.29	1−	2 1/8
		8	16-18	B 75	2	−			
		9	18	76	4	−			
		10	26	77	1	.20	2.49	−1	2 3/8
		11	26	ALT 78	1	−			
		12	79	79	1	.25	3.14	−1	2 3/8
		13	21	80	1	1.05	4.19	−4	2 7/8
		14	}	81	1	−			
		15	}	82	1	−			
		16	41,42,43	E/S 83	4	1.20	5.39	1−2	4 1/8
		17	"	B 83	4	−			
		18	44	*84	2	.50	6.29	1−	5 1/8
		19	}	85	2	−			
		PU	}	86	1	−			
		20	}	87	3	−			
		21	}	88	2,3	−			
		22	43	89		−			
		PU	"	90	1	−			
		23	A42	91	4	.20	6.49	−2	5 3/8
		24	7,8	92	2	.45	7.34	2−4	7 7/8
		25	}	B92	2	−			
		PU	}	93	1	1.01	8.35		
		PU	}	B93	1				
TOTAL		25	17				8:35		7 7/8
FORWARD		91	40				24:11		24 7/8

Figure 6.1

DAILY EDITOR'S LOG

DATE *8/20*   TITLE _____

WORK DAY *4TH*   DIRECTOR _____

PROD. NO. *1560*

CAM ROL	SND ROL	SET	SCENE#	SLATE#	PRINT	TIME	DESCRIPTION
		LIV RM/BEDRM	2-4	71	4	.52	MAST. PAN SEAN X LIV RM TO BEDROOM FIND WOMAN IN BED
		⟩		B71	4		C.U SEAN
		BEDRM	3,4/6	72		.06	MAST. SEAN & CELIA FREEZE SEAN
		⟩		B72	1,2		T2 TO C.U. SEAN
			4	73	1		2 BH - IN BED
		LIV RM	5	74	2	.04	MAST. F.S. DAVE DASH IN FROM BATHROOM TO C.U.
		LIV RM/BEDRM	16-18	E/S 75	2	.48	MAST. SEAN X L-R TO BEDRM - 2/SH SEAN + CHAFFEE
		BEDROOM	⟩	B75	2		OV/SH ON SEAN
		⟩		76	4		OV/SH ON CHAF.
		⟩	26	77	1		MAST. CS CHAF SNORE W/ RAIN FX
		⟩		78	1		ALT. ON 77 - NO RAIN FX
		⟩	19	79	1	.17	MAST. SEAN AWAKES PAN TO LIV RM
		LIV RM/BEDRM	21	80	1	.48	MAST. PAN SEAN X LIV RM TO BEDRM - CHAF ENT. SHOT - HOLD FULL 2/SH
		BEDRM		81	1		C.U SEAN
		⟩		82	1		C.U CHAF
		⟩	41-43	E/S 83	4	1.06	MAST. FS SEAN + BIRD STEW. ENT. DE TO T2/SH
		⟩		B 83	4		STEW EXIT TO LIV RM C.U. SEAN
		BATHRM/BEDRM	44	* 84	2	.43	MAST. MS CHAF COMES THRU DOOR PAN XL-R TO MIRROR - HOLD M 2/SH IN MIRROR
				85	2		C.U SEAN (NO BIRD)
				86	1		PU ON 85
				87	3		C.U CHAF (L) MIRROR SHOT MOVE TO SHOE

WILD TRACKS   REMARKS   (CONT.)
          * 84 MISSLATED 83 TK2

_____
Continuity Supervisor

Figure 6.2

It is imperative to keep the Daily Continuity Log up to the minute. With impeccably kept entries, you will be in a position to answer with alacrity any production-related question that will be asked of you, inevitably at the most frenzied time of your day. Also, your up-to-the-minute records will facilitate the arithmetic necessary for completing the Daily Progress Report. You will be able to promptly hand it to the eager second assistant director.

As you make entries in the Daily Continuity Log, it is advisable to also record the essential data in the Daily Editor's Log (see Figure 6.2). This record has to be submitted to the editing room at the close of each day in order for the assistant film editor to properly assemble the next morning's dailies.

SLATING AUXILIARY
SCENE NUMBERS

The use of auxiliary scene numbers is introduced when only one script-scene number is written while the director *breaks up* the scene with different camera angles and close shots. This aspect is elaborated on in Chapter 10 (also refer to page 87 in this chapter).

Every camera shot mandates a slate number—the only frame of reference the editor has. The creation of auxiliary numbers during filming is unequivocally awarded to the continuity supervisor.

To signify auxiliary numbers, letters of the alphabet are appended to the script-scene number. But be advised that the letters *I* and *O* are never used. It is standard practice in the industry to exclude those letters from script-page numbers and script-scene numbers. The reason is that the letter *I* may be mistaken for the number 1 and the letter *O* may be mistaken for the number 0.

Let us assume that Scene 26 is broken up (covered) with several closer angles. The auxiliary setups will be slated from 26A through 26Z. If additional shots need to be linked to the auxiliary numbers, you will assign such numbers as 26AA, 26AB, 26AC, etc.; then onto 26BA, 26BB, 26BC, and 26CA, 26CB, 26CC, etc.

When announcing slate numbers, the customary way to state the letters of the alphabet is to enunciate names of people, places, or objects that begin with those letters—e.g., Adam, Baker, Charley, David, or Albany, Boston, Chicago, Denver, or apple, banana, cookie, dog. For double letters, you could say Double Adam, Double Baker, Baker Apple, Boston Charlie. (Often, I purposely change the familiar names—e.g., use Cabana for Charlie, Devil for David, and so forth. It breaks up the monotony and assures me that camera and sound are accurately repeating my slate announcements.)

An alternate method of numbering auxiliary shots is as follows: 26x1, 26x2, 26x3, and so forth. For additional setups linked to these numbers, use 26x1A, 26x2A, 26x3A, and so on. This method allows for a wider range of numbers when many setups are involved. The alphabet method sometimes entails the doubling and tripling of letters, which gets clumsy and confusing. Whichever numbering method you prefer, be sure to communicate it to the editor (it might be wise to ask your editors which numbering method *they* prefer). CAUTION: Any auxiliary numbers that you append to a script-scene number in the course of shooting *do not alter* (add to) the original total of the written script scenes (see the section on "Scene Count" under "Daily Progress Report" in Chapter 7).

SLATING EXTRANEOUS SCENES

At times you will be confronted with a script in which extraneous scenes, such as montages, flashbacks, and points of view, are interpolated in the master scene. For a case in point, refer to Chapter 2, page 18. In that scene, the actor verbalizes what is being shown on three projected slides. As mentioned in the earlier chapter, these slide scenes may be transformed into film footage. Script-wise, such integrated scenes are regarded as *auxiliary master scenes*—but they are not construed as "added" script-scene numbers (see CAUTION above).

Let us analyze the short scene example depicted in Chapter 2. By means of dialogue and projected slides, the writer disclosed what may be interpreted cinematically as three montage sequences, but did not provide individual script-scene numbers for them. The omission was compounded by the fact that only one script-scene number (23) was assigned to a three-page episode. This is a shortcoming within the script format. However, as continuity supervisor, you have to be prepared for any predicament. In order to designate the mandated slate numbers for the auxiliary scenes, you are compelled to use the assigned scene number only and append letters of the alphabet to it.

In the above circumstance, I would devise slate numbers such as M23A for the first slide, M23B for the second slide, and M23C for the third slide. The M would stand for *montage*. If the above three story-points were flashbacks, an F would precede the number.

Now, suppose the director covers the auxiliary master shots with two additional setups. For these sequential shots, I'd create the numbers M23AA and M23AB for those of the first slide; M23BA and M23BB for those of the second slide; and M23CA and M23CB for those of the third slide. With this numbering convention, the editor can differentiate the auxiliary-numbered scenes from the original master scenes. The coverage shots on the original master-scene number will be identified by the customary letters of the alphabet and then, if necessary, by double and even triple letters.

NOTE: A complication arises when the numerical slating system is used, because it is not possible to predetermine the numbers of auxiliary shots. Instead, you will have to slate the consecutive number that comes up in rotation. For instance, if in the course of filming script scene 23, you are a slate number 187, then the slate for filming the first slide-shot will be number 188. Any subsequent coverage setups in that sequence will be slated consecutively: 189, 190, etc. Inevitably, the second and third slides will be scheduled for filming days or weeks later. And the slate for those setups will carry the higher consecutive numbers as they come up.

CAUTION: If you are slating numerically, it is imperative that you make notes to the editor, clarifying that slates 188, 189, and 190 belong as montages within the script's master scene 23. Likewise, the later slate numbers assigned to slides 2 and 3 belong to master scene 23. You must be impeccably accurate with your notations regarding the slate numbers so that the editor will have no trouble assembling the disjointed pieces of film into perfect continuity.

SLATING PICTURE WITHOUT SOUND TRACK (MOS)*

When scenes are filmed without corresponding sound tracks, you will state this fact when announcing the slate number. The slate operator will mark the slate MOS (for *without sound track*) or SIL (for *silent*)—both designate a shot without sound track. A properly marked slate spares the editor the worry that a sound track may be missing from a piece of film.

All inserts, trick shots, and slow and fast motion are filmed without sound track. Once again, in your continuity script, Daily Continuity Log and Daily Editor's Log, you must note MOS or SIL alongside the listed slate numbers.

SLATING WILD TRACKS FOR PICTURE

Recorded sound tracks that are not synchronized with the rolling of the camera are called *wild tracks*. Wild tracks are recorded for the "practical" sounds that emanate from a scene, such as a food blender, running water from a faucet, an idling automobile, a running vacuum cleaner, a door slamming, or the sound from any filmed object. These sounds cannot be recorded simultaneously with the camera because they interfere with the dialogue.

It is preferable to record the practical wild tracks while still in the

---

* According to legend, the term MOS originated with a foreign director who once gave the order, "Vee shoot dis mit out sound." A crew member then coined the acronym MOS.

working set; in that way, the *room tone* will be compatible when the film is being edited. (Room Tone is defined under "Definitions of Industry Terms" in Chapter 8.) But it is not always possible, or expedient, to record the practical sounds while in the actual set. Therefore, you should conspicuously note SFX (for *sound effects*) in the right-hand margin of the page at the line where the sound falls in the scene. This will alert the editor to look for a set-recorded sound track or be prepared to order one from a sound library. On the Daily Editor's Log, you should list all the wild tracks that have been recorded that day.

The actual recording may be done at the end of the day, after the camera crew has wrapped. Or a recording session may be scheduled for a future date, at which time all the wild tracks for all the scenes will be done. It is advisable that you keep a list of all the wild tracks indicated in the script, with their respective scene numbers, and give a copy of that list to the editor.

At the recording session, you will inform the sound mixer of the number that corresponds to the filmed shot (complying with the slating method used—either scene numbers or consecutive numbers). The sound mixer "voices" the slate number into the recorder, saying "WT" (for *wild track*) and the number. The property master sets the appropriate appliance or other object in motion, and the desired sound is transmitted onto the tape. When such sound tracks are recorded, you will properly mark your script page by drawing a wiggly line through the words that describe the sound and heading the line with WT and the slate number. This method of marking the script is explained under "The Lined Script" in Chapter 7.

SLATING OFF-CAMERA (OFF-SCREEN) SOUND

Sometimes sounds are written to be intrusions in the scene, e.g., a burst of thunder or lightning, footsteps, sirens, or any extraneous sound. Obviously, such noises cannot be rendered during the shooting of the scene. Instead, either the director or some other person on the stage calls out the "sound" or does a hand-clap when the sound is supposed to be heard in the scene. Again, you must conspicuously note SFX at the point in the scene where the sound should be heard. The editor will subsequently obtain the necessary sound tracks from a sound library and incorporate them at the appropriate places in the film.

SLATING WILD FILM FOOTAGE

Scenes that are not written in the script but are filmed at random, wherever and however they happen, are referred to as *wild footage*. These may be scenes of casual street activity, riots, scenes of disaster, public demonstrations, and so on. Impromptu shots of bystanders' reactions lend an air of spontaneity when cut into conventionally staged scenes.

Wild footage is often filmed with hand-held cameras because there is no time for positioning a camera on a tripod or dolly, or even using a slate. Sometimes shot numbers are voiced because the clapboard isn't handy.

For slating wild footage, employ an arbitrary number for the sequence—say, 300—and precede it with XF (for *extraneous footage*); i.e., XF300, XF301, and so forth.

If XF shots are made without an accompanying sound track, the slate should also be marked MOS. In the haste to get wild footage, scenes may be shot without benefit of slate or sound track. You will then have to confer with the camera personnel and write up a shot description of each scene or subject that has been filmed. Keep a list of wild-footage shots with identifying numbers and dates, and send a copy to the editor.

SLATING WILD SOUND

The term *wild sound* refers to any extraneous sounds that are not relevant to the script and are recorded separate from the camera. Such recordings are usually made during outdoor filming to capture environmental sounds, such as birds chirping, dogs howling, hydraulic machines drilling, brass bands marching, or a helicopter whirling. These sounds will be interspersed in the scenes wherever appropriate during the final editing of the film.

For the slating of wild sound, use consecutive numbers, starting with 1. Advise the sound mixer to precede these numbers with XW (for *extraneous wild sound*)—i.e., XW1, XW2, and so forth. Make a list of the sound-track numbers with a brief description of the sounds recorded; also record the date and place where recorded. Send a copy of the list to the editor (who will of course also receive the sound mixer's report).

SLATING MUSICAL PRODUCTIONS—PLAYBACK

Musical productions or musical numbers interpolated in dramatic scenes are filmed in the same manner as straight action and dialogue scenes, except that the filming is done without sound track (MOS). The songs that are sung and the music for dancing are prerecorded in a recording studio, and the recordings are then *played back* (PL/B) on the sound stage. The singers synchronize (*lip-sync*) their voices and the dancers perform their choreographed routines to the playback music while the camera is filming. This technique was devised to preclude live orchestra accompaniment, which poses huge staging problems and costs. Sometimes even the playing of a musical instrument (piano, violin, guitar, saxophone) is prerecorded, and the actors' hands imitate (fake) the playing when the act is filmed.

The Musical Director usually presides over a musical production in progress. But you too will follow the performance and watch the lip-synching and the coordination of dancing with the playback music. You will receive a copy of the sheet music, giving the title, lyrics, and/or musical score corresponding to each playback record. The bars of music are numbered sequentially. Each record is given a separate PL/B number.

You will announce the scene or shot number and also the PL/B number, to be written on the slate. In like manner, the sound mixer repeats these numbers into the recording panel. This sound track is used only as a guide track—just to give the editor an inkling of what went on during the shooting. The finished film, of course, will carry the properly recorded sound track. In your script notes, be sure to record the PL/B number along with the slate number of every shot.

If there were stops and starts in the performance during a take, you should mark the precise bars of music where these occurred; also, record the timing of each take. And it is advisable for you to check your markings with the musical director for accuracy.

Regarding the picture time of a musical number: you know, of course, that that is predicated on the timing of the prerecorded music. Nevertheless, your script notes should include the timing (and/or the footage) of every take. Such information is often helpful to the editor when cutting the film.

7

"That's a Wrap"

IS THE SEQUENCE COVERED?

Toward the finish of shooting a sequence, the director is likely to ask you, "Am I covered?" You should be able to give the answer without hesitation (The term *coverage* is defined under "What the Continuity Supervisor Oversees" in Chapter 1 and further explained in Chapters 4 and 10.) But you should also quickly refer to the list of shots the director enumerated while blocking and rehearsing the scene. Each shot should have been checked off as it was filmed. Before you give an affirmative answer, make certain that all the cover shots, all the bridge shots (see Chapter 5, page 75), and all the necessary companion angles have been filmed. By the same token, you should be able to tell the director which shots, if any, are needed to complete the sequence.

When all the requisite shots in a scene or a series of scenes have been filmed, the first assistant director announces, "That's a wrap for this set."

STRIKING THE SET

Striking the set means dismantling all the lights and removing all the furnishings. Before the company is about to move out of the set, you must be confident, beyond a doubt, that all components of the scheduled scenes have been filmed. It would be costly indeed to have to reconstruct the set just to film an overlooked bridge shot or close-up.

93

The word *strike* is also used to indicate that a certain character, prop, or action is to be eliminated from the scene. When you hear, "Strike the little girl," "Strike the dog jumping on the chair," "Strike the clock," be assured that no violence is suggested.

COMPANY WRAP

When all the scenes listed on the day's Call Sheet have been shot and covered, or when the time on the clock proclaims the end of the day, the first assistant director shouts, "That's the wrap for today!" That indicates that the day's shooting has come to an end.

The different departments are allotted *wrap time* for gathering up their equipment and preparing whatever daily reports are required for the production office. For the continuity supervisor, this is the time to assemble all the data from your Daily Continuity Log and complete your Daily Progress Report.

DAILY PROGRESS REPORT

At the end of each day, you will give your Daily Progress Report (Figure 7.1) to the second assistant director. You are the only person in the company who controls this essential information. Without your detailed record, the assistant cannot complete the collective data required by the production office. NOTE: You may devise any forms that are convenient for you, so long as the production office receives consistent and accurate information. The sample forms shown in this book embody all the data that the continuity supervisor is required to report.

Following are guidelines for arriving at correct totals.

1. Page Count

Tally the number of pages shot for the day. If company-revised pages have changed the original total page count (by adding or deleting pages), you should use the revised figure. However, if improvisations during shooting have altered (raised or lowered) the total number of pages, you should take page credit only for the original page count as shown in the Shooting Schedule and your Continuity Synopsis/One Line. *Do not revise your breakdown total.* For instance, if the director played a full-page scene down to only half the page and deleted the rest, you must consider the last half of the written page as "covered" (to justify the total page count established in the Shooting Schedule and your One Line). Another term for covered is *credited*. Conversely, if ad libs and extra business extended a half-page scene to a full page or more, do not count the extra material as additional page length. Simply credit only the half-page written in the script.

2. Scene Count

Tally the number of scenes covered. In the course of shooting, if you appended auxiliary scene numbers (A, B, C, etc.) to the written script-scene numbers, do not add the lettered numbers to your original total scene count. You should count (credit) only the script's original scene numbers shot that day (see Chapter 6, under "Slating Auxiliary Scene Numbers"). On the other hand, if company-revised scenes have changed the original total scene count (via additions or deletions), be sure to enter the revised figure under "New Total."

Another consideration in tallying scene count arises when a *comprehensive master shot* is made. That means the director included several script-scene numbers in a single take. You must regard all those scene numbers as covered. For example, slate number 25 encompassed scenes 26, 27, and 28. Therefore, in the column under "Scenes Covered," you will enter scene numbers 25, 26, 27, and 28. In the space under "Shot Today," you will enter the total: 4.

Unfinished scenes. If all the necessary coverage of a scene that includes several script-scene numbers (say 25, 26, 27, and 28) was not completed in one day, you will enter 25, 26, 27, and 28 pt (part) under "Scenes Covered." The total of scenes "Shot Today" will be 3. Then, for as many days as it takes to complete coverage on that series of scene numbers, your Daily Progress Report will list 28 pt under "Scenes Covered." On the day that the coverage is completed, you will write the following under "Scenes Covered": 28 comp (complete). And on that day, under "Shot Today," you will increase the day's total by 1.

3. Setup Count

Tally the number of setups made. Your total will be correct if you have accurately listed a new slate number for every shot. As mentioned earlier, you must announce a new slate number, or a letter appended to a scene (slate) number, every time the camera is repositioned or the lens is changed. Each change counts as a separate setup. And when two or more cameras run simultaneously, each change of camera position and each lens change counts as a separate setup. However—and this is an important caution—when pick-ups have been made within a setup, those shot numbers are excluded from the total. The reason is that neither the camera position nor the lens was changed—only a portion of the shot was repeated, and that does not constitute an additional setup. Another caution in regard to total setups: with consecutive-number slating, be sure to mark PU (for *pick-up*) alongside the numbers that were pick-ups within a shot; do not include the PU numbers in the total of setups (see the numbers listed under "Setups" in the Daily Continuity Log [Chapter 6, Figure 6.1]).

You may wonder why so much emphasis is put on the total of setups. It's a clue for the production office: Is the director's coverage excessive or inadequate for the number of pages shot?

4. Picture-Running Time

Tally the picture-running time for the day. Again, refer to the Daily Continuity Log (Figure 6.1). See how the individual timings (minutes and seconds) are recorded and how the "Total Time" is added up progressively.

DAILIES/RUSHES

In the industry, these interchangeable terms refer to the film that is shot during a given day, sent to the laboratory for printing, and rushed back to the studio the next morning.

All exposed film is printed up as negative footage (*"B" negative*). A technician at the laboratory runs this film throughout the night. The technician simultaneously follows the list of numbers on the Camera Report and notes those that are circled. The circled numbers represent the shots that are to be printed. Then all the pieces of film corresponding to the circled numbers are cut out of the bulk of negative footage, wound on rolls, and processed into positive footage (*"A" negative*).

The day's sound recordings are likewise processed during the night. All printed takes are transferred onto 35mm magnetic track.

The next morning, upon receiving the separate rolls of printed takes of film and sound, the assistant film editor *syncs up* (synchronizes) all the disjointed pieces of film with their respective sound tracks and puts this onto reels. These reels of film and sound are known as the *dailies*.

The dailies are shown in a screening room at the studio for critical viewing by the director, producer, DP, editor, and other key personnel.

With the advent of television, a change in the system of viewing dailies has evolved. In some companies, the day's shoot is put onto video cassettes. Select personnel take them home for viewing. The next day, they communicate their comments to whomever is concerned. This is not yet an industry-wide modus operandi, however, for theatrical films.

DAILY PROGRESS REPORT

Shoot. Call __7:30 A__   Date __8/20__
1st Shot __8:04 A__   Work Day __4TH__
Lunch __1:00 - 2:00 P__   Prod. No. __1560__
1st Shot __2:24 P__   Title _____
Dinner __7:00 - 7:30 P__   Director _____
1st Shot __7:45 P__
Cam. Wrap __8:52__
Snd Wrap __8:52__

	Scenes	Pages	Minutes	Setups
Total Script	60	36 7/8		
Added	1	2/8		
Deleted				
New Total	61	37 1/8		
Shot Prior	23	17	15:36	66
Shot Today	17	7 7/8	8:35	25
Shot To Date	40	24 7/8	24:11	91
Left To Do	21	12 2/8		

Scenes Covered	W/Tracks	Retakes	Remarks
2 19			ADD SC A-42
3 21			
4 26			
5 41			
6 42			
7 43			
8A 44			
16 A-42			
17			
18			

_____
Continuity Supervisor

Figure 7.1

CONTINUITY NOTES TO THE EDITOR

At the end of each day's shoot, you will make photocopies of both your left-hand and right-hand script pages (see pages 104–113). Those copies, together with the Daily Editor's Log, have to be turned in to the editor at the end of each shooting day.

The notes in your continuity script pages must be clear and comprehensible. If you do not have neat handwriting, you should print or type your information.

> NOTE: Never send the editor the original pages from your book. These must always remain in your possession.

The routine of daily photocopies to the editor came into practice with the advent of television and, of course, the advent of copying machines. Because shooting for television is done at a much faster pace than for feature films, editors need the pages as quickly as possible to hasten the assembling and editing of the film. While the shooting of feature pictures is supposedly less hectic, the routine of daily photocopies to the editor prevails.

Pages often get messy because of the myriad changes that are made during shooting. You should tidy these pages before photocopying them. If your pages become illegible, you should get clean script pages and neatly rewrite all the original continuity data, as well as all rulings and special notations. (If photocopying equipment is not available, you will have to transfer everything onto fresh script pages in handwriting, printing, or type.) Inasmuch as you are the line of communication between the stage and the editor, it is mandatory that your notes be easily readable. It saves valuable editing time (and company expense) if the editor is spared laborious effort in deciphering incomprehensible handwriting.

The Left-hand Script Page

You will record the following information on the left-hand page of the script:

- ☐ Shot descriptions
- ☐ Slate numbers
- ☐ Dates of shots
- ☐ Take numbers

☐ Running time of each take; noted complete or incomplete

☐ Reason for not printing takes

☐ Lens sizes

☐ Camera and Sound roll numbers (if required)

The standard code for abbreviations is as follows:

NG (no good)

NGD (no good for dialogue)

NGC (no good for camera)

NGS (no good for sound)

COMP–HOLD (good, but not yet for printing)

INC (incomplete—NG or good to the break; speech number)

CIRCLE around a number indicates that this take, whether complete or incomplete, is to be printed.

All the data on the left-hand page of the script provide the editor with easy reference to the content of each shot. Without this detailed information, the editor would have to spend considerable time and effort going through voluminous strips of film to locate a needed shot for viewing on the Moviola.

An essential detail on the left-hand page—the recorded timing of each take—enables the editor to quickly select a necessary *out take* (see "Out Takes" section of Chapter 5).

I found a practical measure that saves precious moments and enhances efficiency when shooting become hectic. During prep time, I rule all the left-hand pages into three vertical sections. The first section is for slate numbers, take and print numbers, and the timings; also, dates of the shots. The second section is for the shot descriptions, lens sizes, and camera and sound-roll numbers (if required). The third section is reserved for special notations on such things as set diagrams, camera positions, and details of action, props, and wardrobe.

IMPORTANT: Make conspicuous notations in the third section, as well as in the margin of the right-hand script page, of any *mismatches* that you called attention to but that the director asserted were not important enough to retake. These notations will protect you from undue blame later. They will also give the editor the opportunity to judiciously cut around the mismatches, thus saving valuable editing time.

The Right-hand Script Page/
The Lined Script

You will record the following information on the right-hand page of the script:

☐ Notations of any deviations from the written script in dialogue or action that occurred during the performance.

☐ Marginal notes of any disruptions in the scene, such as off-camera noises or on-camera overlaps; also notes on which cover shots eliminate the interferences.

☐ Markings at the exact spots on the page where inserts will appear in the film, such as a picture, a letter, the time on a clock, a gun, a book title, or a newspaper headline.

☐ Markings at the exact spots on the page where sound effects (SFX) occur in the scene, such as a phone ringing, a door slamming, a baby crying, the sound of off-screen hammering, footsteps, thunder, sirens, and the like.

☐ Perpendicular lines, which are the editor's blueprint for cutting the film. The lines drawn on the script page, marked with their identifying captions (slate numbers) account for each setup made. The procedure is simple. At the start of each shot, draw the perpendicular line from the slate number down to the exact spot where the shot ends. At this point, draw a small horizontal line or a tick to mark the end of the shot. If the shot continues to subsequent pages, place an arrow on the line at the bottom of the page; then repeat the slate number with an arrow at the top of the next page, draw the line down to the finish of the shot, and place the tick there. All succeeding pages should be treated likewise.

☐ The *wiggly line* always evokes the question, "What is the significance of the wiggly line?" The explanation is simple. A straight line is drawn through those speeches and actions that have been filmed, while a wiggly line is drawn through any off-camera dialogue or sound. This simple pattern provides the editor with a quick reference as to which characters are speaking on-camera and which are off. It also helps you to quickly spot off-camera dialogue that may need to be filmed.

☐ When a shot is interrupted (cut) before completion, draw the perpendicular line and the tick to the spot in the dialogue or business where that take stopped. (At this point, the reason for *numbering speeches* suggested in Chapter 4 becomes apparent.) If you cannot take the time to immediately draw the line during hectic shooting, jot down the number of the speech alongside the take. In a calmer moment, you can draw the line; the speech number lets you know how far the take went. (You will not find speech numbering in the sample teleplay included in this book, because shooting was quite normal.)

For continuation of the shot, place a new slate number at the starting point of the pick-up and add the letters PU (for *pick-up*) to the number; then continue the line to the end of the shot. Frequently, several pick up shots will be filmed before the scene is completed.

☐ When multiple cameras are used, draw the perpendicular and wiggly lines in the same manner for each camera, and designate at each slate number which camera applies—A, B, or C. Draw those lines adjacent to the A-camera line. Lines for pick-up shots are drawn in the same manner as for the single camera (see the Final Continuity Script, Figure 7.3).

Production Stock Shots

There will be times when the principal photography unit will be required to shoot certain scenes as STOCK SHOTS. This is most apt to happen when shooting episodic television.

When the company shoots stock shots (usually without a script), it is your responsibility to write a comprehensive description of each scene. Number the shots consecutively, starting with 1, and precede each number with an S (see Figure 7.2). The slates should also read S-1, S-2, and so on. Attach this dated record to your continuity script and send copies to the editor and the production office.

PRODUCTION STOCK SHOTS

TITLE:_____   DATE:_____

SLATE #

S-1   EXT. MEDICAL BLDG - DAY.
            Unmarked blue Ford pulls up to curb L-R,
50 ft.   stops. Smith driving, Jones alongside.
            Both get out, PAN their walk across side-
            walk, and HOLD as they go into the building.

S-2   EXT. MEDICAL BLDG - DAY
            Unmarked blue Ford parked at curb R-L.
50 ft.   Smith behind wheel, Jones alongside. Both
            get out. PAN their walk R-L. EXIT into
            the building. PAN UP along front of build-
            ing and HOLD on sculptured Medical Insignia.

S-3   EXT. MEDICAL BLDG -DAY
            Start UP ANGLE on Medical Insignia - PAN
50 ft.   DOWN to Long Shot of Street. Blue unmarked
            Ford parked at curb R-L. Smith is behind
            wheel, Jones alongside. Both get out and
            EXIT into the building.

S-4   EXT. MEDICAL BLDG - NITE
            Start UP ANGLE on Medical Insignia (as
75 ft.   above), PAN DOWN front of building to
            Long Shot on entrance doors. Smith and
            Jones come out of building and cross to
            parked car at curb (R-L). They get into
            car: Smith at wheel, Jones alongside.
            Start motor and drive away R-L.

                 Tk-1 Camera late panning.
                 Smith did not start motor.

                 Tk-2 Okay

Figure 7.2

FINAL LINED CONTINUITY SCRIPT

You have seen, first, the original writer's script (Chapter 2, Figure 2.1), then the same script with the continuity supervisor's breakdown notes (Chapter 2, Figure 2.2). The following is the final lined continuity script—a composite record of what has been put on film. This is the editor's bible.

The sample script presented here represents a shoot using consecutive-number slating and, occasionally, two cameras. Notice how the perpendicular lines are drawn. The format conveys to the editor that there is a length of film for each line, and it also conveys who and what is on-camera and who and what is off-camera.

The last three pages are samples of the Wardrobe Outline related to this shoot. It is not necessary to submit these pages to the editor, but they should be appended to your work script.

1	8/13 Sc. 1	
① comp. .12	Master - F.S. on door Sean enters R-L, opens door with Key - exits to inside	
71 A/B	8/20 Sc. 2, 3, 4/6	

① Comp.   .45
   poor A-CAM
   good B-CAM
2 - FS
3 - Comp .44
   NG B-CAM
④ Comp.   .52
	Master - Start F.S. angle on
	living room side door -
	Sean enters from behind
	drape - drops hat + bag -
	Pan him X- living room
	L-R to bedroom (thru open
	door) DI with his walk to
	bed - Hold Sgle M.S. as he
	removes his clothes - Pan R
	as he gets into bed, then
	ZO to reveal Tite/2 Sean
	+ Celia in bed - She exits
	frame R - Hold CS Sean
	
	   B-CAM: CU Sean
	        standing at bed
		Shirt
		pants
		etc
		L sh
		R sh
		L st
		R st

72 A/B*	8/20 Sc. 3, 4/6 FREEZE FRAME	

1 - Comp cr.or .16
   ngc
② camp   cr .06
   * PRINT 1 + 2
     B-CAM
	Med. 2/Sh in bed - overlap
	"I love you" - Sean
	springs up - FREEZE - then
	exit shot L
	   B-CAM: Tite/2 then ZI to
	       CU Sean	

73	8/20 Sc. 4	
① Comp .14	2 BIG HEADS in bed	
74	8/20 Sc. 5	
1 - Comp .07 ② Comp cr .04	Master - F.S. toward Bath- room - door slides open - slave rushes fwd cam to CU - Look off L - dialog	

Figure 7.3

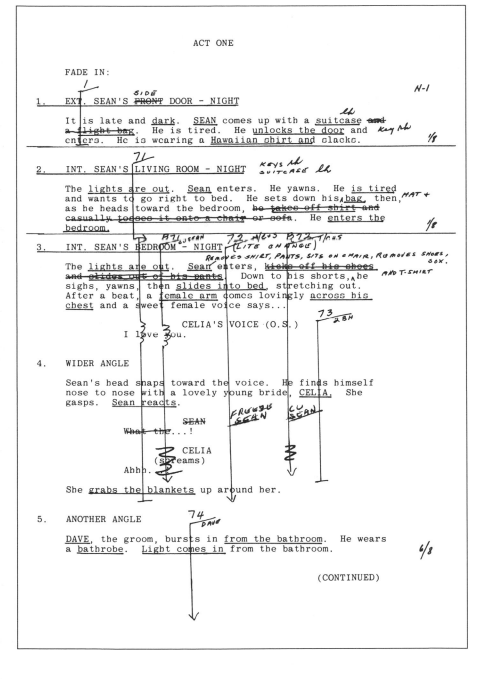

ACT ONE

FADE IN:

1. EXT. SEAN'S ~~FRONT~~ *SIDE* DOOR - NIGHT   N-1

    It is late and <u>dark</u>. <u>SEAN</u> comes up with a <u>suitcase</u> ~~and~~
    ~~a flight bag~~. He is tired. He <u>unlocks the door</u> and *key nh*
    enters. He is wearing a <u>Hawaiian shirt and</u> slacks.   1/8

2. INT. SEAN'S LIVING ROOM - NIGHT *KEYS nh SUITCASE lh*

    The <u>lights are out</u>. <u>Sean</u> enters. He yawns. He <u>is tired</u>
    and wants to go right to bed. He sets down his <u>bag</u>, then, *HAT +*
    as he heads toward the bedroom, ~~he takes off shirt and~~
    ~~casually tosses it onto a chair~~ or ~~sofa~~. He <u>enters the</u>
    <u>bedroom</u>.   1/8

3. INT. SEAN'S BEDROOM - NIGHT *(LITE CHANGE)*

    REMOVES SHIRT, PANTS, SITS ON CHAIR, REMOVES SHOES, SOX,
    The <u>lights are out</u>. <u>Sean</u> enters, ~~kicks off his shoes~~ *AND T-SHIRT*
    ~~and slides out of his pants~~. Down to his shorts, he
    sighs, yawns, then <u>slides into bed</u>, stretching out.
    After a beat, a female arm comes lovingly <u>across his</u>
    <u>chest</u> and a sweet female voice says...

                    CELIA'S VOICE (O.S.)   73
                                                          2BH
            I <u>love you</u>.

4. WIDER ANGLE

    Sean's head snaps toward the voice. He finds himself
    nose to nose with a lovely young bride, <u>CELIA</u>. She
    gasps. <u>Sean reacts</u>.

                    ~~SEAN~~   *FREEZE   CU*
            ~~What the...!~~   *SEAN   SEAN*

                    CELIA
                    (screams)
            Ahhh.

    She <u>grabs the blankets</u> up around her.

5. ANOTHER ANGLE   74
                             DAVE
    <u>DAVE</u>, the groom, bursts in <u>from the bathroom</u>. He wears
    a <u>bathrobe</u>. <u>Light comes in</u> from the bathroom.   6/8

                                        (CONTINUED)

92 $\frac{2}{8}$	8/20 Sc. 7, 8	

1- Inc ngd .45
② Inc + P.U. .45
	Master - Tite Group 4/Sh
	Moe - Dean - Celia - Dave
	(2nd stool
	at bar
	Gruber enters thru front
	door to 5/Sh - on cue Moe
	Xes Fg to C R - 5/Sh
	Dean - Gruber - Celia - Dave - Moe
	dialog - on cue, Dean
	rises
	   B-CAM: Tite/2
	        Celia/Dave	

96	8/21 Sc. 7, 8	
① comp .58	Close/2: Moe & Dean R. profiles - Moe exits shot R - Hold C U Dean (R)	
97	8/21 Sc. 8	
① comp. 1.43	C U Gruber - enters thru front door - dialog to end of scene.	

2.

5 (Cont.)   *7th DAVE*   *N-1*

                    DAVE
          Baby, what is it?

B71 SEAN   *72 M/CvS*   *B72 CU SEAN*

6.   ANGLE ON SEAN

     He is halfway out of bed, still not certain what this is all
     about. He whips his head around to look towards the new voice.
     It has all happened in a split second. We FREEZE FRAME
     catching him in an awkward position, halfway out of bed.   *7/8*

                                              CUT TO:

92 MAST   *B92 CEL & DAVE*

7.   INT. SEAN'S LIVING ROOM - NIGHT *(LATER THAT NIGHT)*   *N-14*

     SEATED AT BAR
     Sean, Celia and Dave are there in robes. MOE is there in
     uniform. Dave is holding his arm protectively around Celia.

                    96 MOE & SEAN
                    MOE *(HOLDING POLICE CARD) Rh*
          You wanna press charges, Doc?

                    DAVE   *NOTE TO EDITOR*
          What do you mean? He attacked   *USE COVERAGE AND*
          my wife.   *O.S. LINES TO COVER*
                                                  NG MASTER SOUND.
                    MOE
               (to Sean) *I GOT*
          Sorry, Doc...it's my duty to
          inform you of your rights. *YOU HAVE*
          THE RIGHT TO REMAIN SILENT...
                    SEAN
          I didn't attack her. I just got
          in bed with her. *IT'S MY BED.*

8.   ANGLE ON FRONT DOOR   *97 GRU*

                    keys
     MRS. GRUBER lets herself in. Celia comes up to her.   *@ CURLERS*
                                                                IN HAIR
                    CELIA   *YOU'RE HERE.*
          Mrs. Gruber, thank goodness. Will
          you tell them you rented it to us?
          They don't believe us.

                    GRUBER
               (sees Sean)
          What are you doing here?

                    SEAN
          I live here.

                                         (CONTINUED)   *6/8*

93 $\frac{A}{B}$	8/20 Sc. 8	
① comp. + P.U. ev. 1.01	P.U. on 92 A + B	
98	8/21 Sc 8	
1- Inc nga .10 2- Inc ngs .18 3- Inc nga .76 ④ comp + P.U. 2.07	C.U. Moe (L)	
94 $\frac{A}{B}$	8/20 Sc 8	
1- Inc ngd .15 ② comp + PU .50	P.U. on 93 A + B	

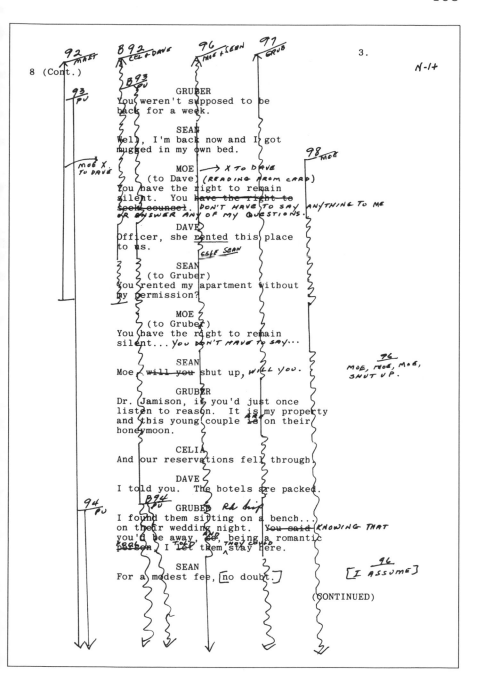

3.

8 (Cont.)

92 MAST   B 92 CELE + DAVE   96 MOE + SEAN   97 GRUB

N-14

93 PU

B 93 PU

98 MOE

GRUBER
You weren't supposed to be
back for a week.

SEAN
Well, I'm back now and I got
mugged in my own bed.

MOE X.
TO DAVE

MOE → X TO DAVE
(to Dave) (READING FROM CARD)
You have the right to remain
silent. You have the right to
speak counsel. DON'T HAVE TO SAY ANYTHING TO ME
OR ANSWER ANY OF MY QUESTIONS.

DAVE
Officer, she rented this place
to us.

CELE SEAN

SEAN
(to Gruber)
You rented my apartment without
my permission?

MOE
(to Gruber)
You have the right to remain
silent... YOU DON'T HAVE TO SAY...

SEAN
Moe, will you shut up, WILL YOU.

MOE,
MOE, MOE, MOE,
SHUT UP.

GRUBER
Dr. Jamison, if you'd just once
listen to reason. It is my property
and this young couple is on their
honeymoon.

CELIA
And our reservations fell through.

DAVE
I told you. The hotels are packed.

94 PU

B 94 PU

GRUBER Rd hip
I found them sitting on a bench...
on their wedding night. You said KNOWING THAT
you'd be away, and being a romantic
person I let them stay here.
THEY COULD

SEAN
For a modest fee, [no doubt.]

96
[I ASSUME]

(CONTINUED)

95 A/B	8/20	Sc. 8	
① Comp	.23	P.V. on 94 A + B	
99	8/21	Sc 8	
① Comp.	.08	P.V. on 98 C U mae's last line	
51	8/17	Sc. 9	
1- Comp. ② Comp.	.71 .22	Master - F.S. angle thru patio, past Puni at counter - Chaffee enters from Lbg patio, xing to Puni. Med. 2/sh. Chaffee + Puni dialog - Chaffee exits to corridor Bgk - ZI to C.S. Puni - she picks up flowers + exits past C.R.	

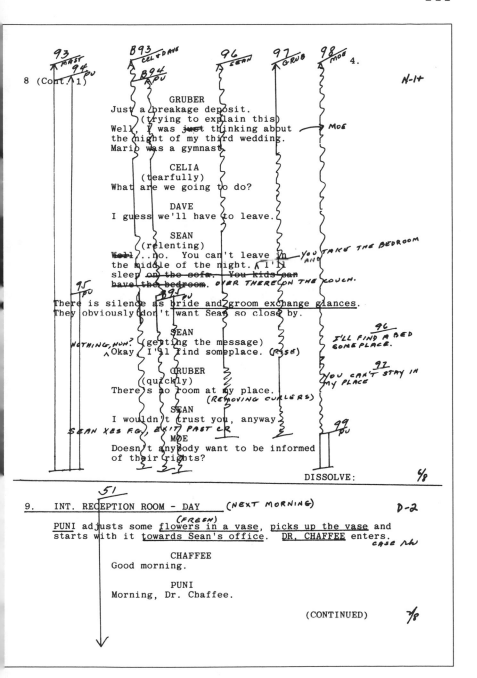

93 · MAST
94 · PU
8 (Cont'd 1)

B93 · CEL & DAVE
B94 · PU

96 · SEAN

97 · GRUB

98 · MOE   4.

N-1+

GRUBER
Just a breakage deposit.
(trying to explain this)
Well, I was ~~just~~ thinking about → MOE
the night of my third wedding.
Mario was a gymnast.

CELIA
(tearfully)
What are we going to do?

DAVE
I guess we'll have to leave.

SEAN
(relenting)
~~Well~~..no. You can't leave in → YOU TAKE THE BEDROOM
the middle of the night. ~~I'll~~   AND
~~sleep on the sofa. You kids can~~
~~have the bedroom.~~ OVER THERE ON THE COUCH.

95 · PU

B95 · PU

There is silence as bride and groom exchange glances.
They obviously don't want Sean so close by.

NOTHING, NOW?   SEAN
                    (getting the message)
        Okay, I'll find someplace. (RISE)

96
I'LL FIND A BED
SOMEPLACE.

GRUBER
(quickly)
There's no room at my place.
        (REMOVING CURLERS)

97
YOU CAN'T STAY IN
MY PLACE

SEAN
I wouldn't trust you, anyway.

SEAN XES F.G., EXIT PAST CR

99 · PU

MOE
Doesn't anybody want to be informed
of their rights?

DISSOLVE: 4/8

51

9.   INT. RECEPTION ROOM - DAY   (NEXT MORNING)   D-2
        (FRESH)
PUNI adjusts some flowers in a vase, picks up the vase and
starts with it towards Sean's office. DR. CHAFFEE enters.
                                                CASE NW

CHAFFEE
Good morning.

PUNI
Morning, Dr. Chaffee.

(CONTINUED)   7/8

112

50	8/16 Sc. 10,11	
1- Inc nge .12 2- Comp mgs .23 ③ comp .22	Master - Start M.S. on screen - Puni comes thru - Pan her X L-R to desk + reveal Sean asleep on sofa - she xes to him - Z I to Site/2 shs Sean awakens - dialog.	

5.

9 (Cont.)   D-2

51

TO F.G.   CHAFFEE
            Puni, I've told you and told you...
            stop putting flowers around.

                      PUNI
            But Doctor, this is Hawaii.

                      CHAFFEE
            I don't care. They're full of
            pollen. They'll make my patients
            sneeze.

He exits into the corridor. Puni looks after him and
makes a face.

                      PUNI *(IMITATES HIM)*
            ~~Yankee, go home.~~
            MAKE MY PATIENTS SNEEZE... ACHOO!
EXITS TO SEAN'S OFFICE.   CUT TO: 3/8

───

50   D-2

10.   INT. SEAN'S OFFICE - DAY *(MORNING)*

      Puni enters and sets the vase of flowers on his desk.

11.   ANOTHER ANGLE

      Sean, wearing a rumpled sport shirt and pants, is stirring
      on the sofa where he apparently has spent the night.

                      PUNI
            Dr. Jamison, what are you doing
            here?

                      SEAN
                 (stretches, feels back)
            I've been asking myself that all
            night.
                 (rubs back again)
            Ohhh...
                 (gets up)

                      PUNI
            But, Doctor, why couldn't you
            sleep in your own bed?

                      SEAN
            It was two against one...

      Puni reacts.

                                      CUT TO: 1/8

WARDROBE OUTLINE

TITLE _____   Time Breakdown _N-1_

Scene Nos.	Sets	Date Shot
1	EXT SEAN ~~FRONT~~ SIDE DOOR	8/13
2	SEAN LIVING ROOM	8/20
3, 4	⎧ SEAN BEDROOM	8/20
5	⎨ ANGLE BATHROOM (LITE)	8/20
6	⎩ SEAN BEDROOM	8/20

CHARACTERS

SEAN
Straw hat. navy feather
Blu/wh check west Shirt
(inside navy denim
pants)
fringy west. belt
  SC3: T-shirt
        ~~striped~~ shorts

DAVE
yellow paj

CELIA
Pink Baby-Doll nightie
wedding ring

WARDROBE OUTLINE

TITLE _____ Time Breakdown _N-1-(LATER)_

Scene Nos.   Sets   Date Shot
_7, 8_   _SEAN LIVING ROOM_   _8/21_
_____   _____   _____
_____   _____   _____
_____   _____   _____
_____   _____   _____
_____   _____   _____
_____   _____   _____

CHARACTERS

SEAN	CELIA
Same as next page (T. Shirt under robe)	Same as previous page + short lace robe Hair on R shld wedding ring

DAVE	GRUBER
Same as previous page + short green terry robe	west. shirt (patched cuffs open over lt blu paj. pants curlers in hair

MOE	
Uniform wear hat- strap down R.S.	

WARDROBE OUTLINE

TITLE _____   Time Breakdown _D-2_

Scene Nos.	Sets	Date Shot
9	RECEPTION ROOM	8/17
10, 11	SEAN OFFICE	8/16

CHARACTERS

SEAN
Red/wh print short robe
Barefoot
Sc. 10: no T-shirt under robe

CHAFFEE
charc. silk suit
Blu shirt
Gold/red pattern tie

PUNI
Lavender + wh print
chamsong over wh pants
Violets in hair R.S.

At this point, I would like to direct your attention to the Daily Continuity Log (Chapter 6, Figure 6.1). Compare it with the Lined Continuity Script. You will discern that the shooting of Scenes 7 and 8 came 21 setups after shooting Scenes 2 through 6 (per the consecutive-number slating). You will realize, of course, that the reproduced page of the Continuity Log does not reflect the entire day's work. As an expedient measure—and in order for you to get an overall picture of a finished Daily Continuity Log—I totaled the page as though it were the end of that day. For the same reason, I carried those totals over to the Daily Progress Report (Figure 7.1) so you can envision that completed report. Also, refer to the Daily Editor's Log (Chapter 6, Figure 6.2); that page reflects only a small part of the day's shoot. I believe that the above-mentioned samples are explanatory enough to enable you to comprehend and follow the formats—or to improvise whatever forms will be easiest for you. When beginning any assignment, it's a good idea to ask the assistant director and editor what manner of records they prefer—and oblige them.

CLEANUP TIME*

It is customary to be allotted time at the end of the shooting schedule to *clean up* your script. That entails making a neat, comprehensive body of notes for the editor, either written or typed. Depending on the daily work load, you can sometimes accomplish a bit of cleaning up or typing of notes during long waits while sets are being erected or elaborately lit. But this is not likely to happen in television. And typing of notes for television shows is not necessary unless the company requires it; clean photocopies are adequate.

The amount of cleanup time you will need at the end of a shooting schedule will vary; this is a matter to be discussed with the production manager.

---

* It is advisable to include in your deal memo that cleanup time will be paid in addition to daily wrap time, since the latter is spent preparing daily reports.

8

Film Language

The preceding chapters delineate the continuity supervisor's role with respect to breaking down a script and recording the activities of a day's shoot—all focused on your important relationship with the editor and the production office. The remaining chapters introduce technological elements of filming and the creative aspects of your important relationship with the director.

But before we proceed, I would like to familiarize you with a partial list of industry terms (many are further explained in the book). Instead of a routine glossary at the end of the book, I prefer to include definitions of terms within the text. In that way, the designations are an integral part of film education to extend your vocabulary as a practicing continuity supervisor.

This book does not purport to provide definitive explanations on all the jargon related to film production. There are innumerable source books to be found in libraries and bookstores.

DEFINITIONS OF INDUSTRY TERMS

"A" Negative Film that has been processed at the laboratory (i.e., the printed takes).

Academy The term refers to the standard aperture size for framing a picture to be viewed via a 35mm camera in a movie theatre. The ratio is the standard guideline set by the Academy of Motion Picture Arts and

119

Sciences. Pictures for television viewing are held at a slightly reduced ratio (known as the TV cutoff). You will hear the operator say "It's in the Academy." This calls for a small adjustment in the framing (e.g., repositioning the camera, changing the lens focal length, or adjusting the lighting).

Academy of Motion Picture Arts and Sciences (AMPAS) The organization of professionals in the motion picture industry. Membership is by invitation only. The members vote annually for the current year's highest achievements in the crafts, for which the Oscar statuette is awarded.

Action 1. The director's command for the performance to begin. 2. Any movement in a scene being filmed.

ADR The abbreviation for Automated Dialogue Replacement—a technical procedure used when dialogue is added to silent film during postproduction.

Aerial Shot A scene shot from the air through a camera placed inside a helicopter or an airplane.

AFI The abbreviation for the American Film Institute, a special school that was founded for the establishment of an educational program for professional filmmakers.

Ambient (Atmosphere) Sound Track The recording of the nebulous natural background and atmospheric sounds inherent in a scene. This recording is made for indoor as well as outdoor sets. After a scene has been filmed, the sound mixer has the assistant director (AD) call for absolute silence on the stage, then turns on the recorder to capture the atmospheric substance that permeates the set. This special track provides the editor with sound continuity in cases where sound variances occur during filming, or sound gaps occur between match cuts. These gaps create unnatural silences in portions of the film. Therefore the editor lays in pieces of ambient track to complement the shots.

AMPTP The abbreviation for American Motion Picture and Television Producers. The membership comprises motion picture and television producers who establish programs and codes for industry employees.

Angle The field of view (perspective of a lens) from the position of the camera when filming. *Normal angle* places the camera at eye level. *Low angle* places the camera in a lowered position, shooting upward. *High angle* (also called *Down angle*) places the camera in an elevated position, shooting downward. *Wide angle* encompasses a large area and holds full figures. *Medium angle* encompasses a smaller area and holds figures approximately from the waist up. *Close angle* (or *Close-up*) holds a magnified portion of a figure or an object.

Answer Print The laboratory's first composite print of the film footage and sound track for critical viewing by the powers that be.

A-Page A page added to the script. Letters are appended to the page number (e.g., 21A comes between 21 and 22, but page A21 precedes page 21).

Apple Box   A wooden four-sided object of varying size that is used to elevate a person or an object to required height for camera angles. When upended, the box serves as a seat.

Arc Light   A special lamp of high intensity. It is often used to simulate daylight when shooting a scene at night that takes place in the daytime (called *night-for-day shooting*).

Arc Out   The instruction to an actor to walk in a curved line rather than a straight line. The former makes for better camera composition. See *Banana Walk*.

Arriflex   The trade name for a portable hand-held camera; also called *Arri*.

A-Scene   A scene added to the script or added during shooting (e.g., Scenes 21A and 21B precede Scene 22; Scenes A21 and B21 precede Scene 21).

Atmosphere   1. The subtle aura pervading a scene. 2. People in a scene other than the principal actors (*extras*).

Audio   Any element of sound in film and television.

Aura   See *Atmosphere*.

"B" Negative   Refers to takes on film that have not been printed. See *"A" Negative*.

Backdrop/Backing   1. A large piece of scenery—e.g., a painting or photograph—used as an artificial background during the filming of a scene when the view through a window in the set is supposed to be a landscape or a street with buildings. 2. Any facsimile used for background purposes.

Background Presence   See *Ambient (Atmosphere) Sound Track*.

Banana Walk   Denotes walking in a curved line. This term was inspired by the shape of a banana. See *Arc Out*.

Barn Doors   Flaps that are hinged to camera lights. Adjustment of the flaps regulates the amount and the shapes of light that falls onto the set.

Barney   A special cover over the camera that insulates the camera noise.

Beat   A deliberate slight pause in the flow of dialogue or action.

Big Head Close-up   The frame holds the subject's face from chin to top of head.

Bit   A conspicuous minor part in a film.

Blimp   See *Barney*.

Bloop   1. The noise made when two pieces of sound track are spliced. A patch is affixed to eliminate the sound. 2. The device used to delete any undesirable words or sounds, such as frequently occur in live television. (You'll hear the expression, "That'll have to be blooped.")

Blooper   A mistake or a fluff made in dialogue or action during filming.

Boom Camera   A camera mounted on a hydraulically operated apparatus that permits smooth vertical camera movements—upward and downward—for shots of continuous action when characters stand from a seated position or vice versa.

Boom Mike   The microphone attached to the apparatus of the sound boom.

Breakaway Props   Articles made of special material that can be shattered or broken apart without injuring the participants in a scene.

Bridge Shot   Any extraneous shot that connects two pieces of cut film.

Brute   An extra large camera light. See *Arc Light.*

Cameo   A small part in a film, performed by a distinguished actor.

Camera Left   Subjects or objects are positioned at the left side of the frame or move toward the left side of the frame. Screen direction is opposite to legitimate stage direction. As you view the scene in front of the camera, Camera Left is parallel to your left-hand side. To move Camera Left, a performer moves in the direction of his or her *right-hand side;* to move Stage Left, a performer moves in the direction of his or her *left-hand side.*

Camera Right   The opposite of Camera Left. As you view the scene in front of the camera, Camera Right is parallel to your right-hand side. To move Camera Right, a performer moves in the direction of his or her *left-hand side;* to move Stage Right, a performer moves in the direction of his or her *right-hand side.*

Camera Run Out   Signifies that the magazine of film is empty before the finish of a shot.

Catwalk   A wooden walkway suspended above the stage set to accommodate personnel handling lighting and other equipment. Another term for scaffold.

Choker   The frame holds a face from the neck up.

Clapboard   See *Slate.*

Close Shot   The frame holds the subject's figure from ribs to top of head.

Close-up   The frame holds the subject's figure from shoulders to top of head; a magnified image of an object.

Cookie   See *Cukaloris.*

Cover Set   1. A standby set inside the sound stage, to be used when inclement weather or other factors prevent the shooting of an outdoor set. 2. A set prepared for use in case of any emergency.

Cover Shot   An extra shot made to use in case it becomes necessary to cut out a questionable piece of film or to cover up a mismatch in continuity.

Crab Dolly   A small vehicle equipped with special wheels designed to move in all directions—forward, backward, and sideways (like a crab, from which its name is derived). During filming, the camera and operator are stationed on the dolly, and the camera is mounted on a hydraulically operated apparatus (see *Boom Camera*). The combination of adjustable wheels and the camera's flexibility facilitates the shooting of multiple actions within a scene.

Crane Shot   A scene filmed from an extreme height. The camera is mounted on a large, specially constructed vehicle known as a *crane.* A hydraulically operated apparatus permits the raising of the camera for filming. A camera mounted on a crane has extraordinary maneuverability and is capable of panning 360°.

Credits   The list of names acknowledging the persons and craftspeople involved in the production of a motion picture or television film. The list appears either before or after the presentation.

Cross Angle   The frame holds two or more subjects, with the camera focused on (shooting past) the profiles at either camera left (CL) or camera right (CR).

Crosses   Movements of subjects from one place to another in a scene, crossing the screen left to right or right to left.

Cross Cutting   A method of editing wherein two or more scenes that occur at different locales are assembled alternately (*intercut*) to show that the different actions are taking place simultaneously, or wherein scenes that occur in different time frames are intercut. Also called *parallel action*.

Cue Cards   Large cardboard sheets from which actors read written dialogue and/or directions (sometimes referred to, humorously, as *idiot cards*). Another device used for this purpose is the mechanical Tele-Prompter.

Cue Tracks   Sound recordings that are synchronized with the rolling of the camera but are used only as guide tracks. Often, when shooting outdoors, atmospheric interferences (overhead airplanes, background disturbances) render a scene's dialogue unusable. Subsequently, the actors rerecord the dialogue onto a clean sound track, and the off-screen (OS) noises are edited in perspective.

Cukaloris   A piece of plywood or plastic with cutout patterns of varying shapes and sizes that casts surface shadows onto the set when placed in front of a light source. Also called a *cookie*.

Cut   This term has several filmic interpretations. 1. In editing: (a) to sever a segment of film and join it to another segment of film (to *splice*); (b) to immediately change from one shot to another; (c) to delete (cut out) a portion of a shot. 2. In directing: the order that the director gives to stop the action of a performance or the operation of any camera or sound equipment. 3. In the script: to delete any action or dialogue from the written page.

Cutaway   A shot that is interjected in a scene within the flow of the scene's immediate action. It may be a relevant story accent, an intentional distraction, or a cover-up for a mismatch.

Cutter   1. An assistant film editor who assembles the dailies and prepares the film for viewing. 2. The device used to cut down a shaft of light (see *Barn Doors; Gobo; Scrim*).

Cutting Room   The room that houses the equipment used in assembling and editing the processed film. The film is viewed on an apparatus called the *Moviola*. There are also contemporary machines that expedite film editing, manufactured under various trade names. The latest editing process uses laser technology.

Dailies   Reels of processed film from the laboratory that comprise the previous day's shoot. This film is viewed by the director, the producer, and other concerned personnel.

Day-for-Night Denotes the filming of an exterior nighttime scene during the daytime. Special filters are attached to the lens to create darkness.

Depth of Field The distance between the camera lens and the subjects being filmed when the foreground and background are equally in focus.

DGA Abbreviation for Directors Guild of America.

Dialogue All the words spoken by actors during filming.

Dissolve The process whereby an image on the screen begins to disappear as another image takes its place. The term denotes the transition from one scene to another, or the end of a sequence. The process is executed at an optical laboratory. Some cameras have the technical capability to effect a dissolve.

Dolly A platform with wheels, onto which a camera on a tripod is fastened. This makes it possible to move the camera forward and backward to follow the action. See *Crab Dolly.*

Dolly Back The camera is pulled backward, away from the subjects or objects, and thus moves from a closer to a wider angle. This makes the images appear smaller on the screen.

Dolly In The camera is pushed forward, toward the subjects, and thus moves from a wider to a closer angle. This makes the images appear larger on the screen.

Dolly Shot Any shot in which the action is followed with a camera on wheels.

Dolly Tracks Rails that are laid down to accommodate the wheels of a dolly used for a moving shot.

Double 1. The person who substitutes for a principal actor *(stunts)*. 2. Duplication of an article of props or wardrobe.

Down Angle Shooting downward on a scene. See *Boom Camera: Crane Shot.*

Downstage The area closest to the camera. Moving downstage means moving toward the *foreground* (FG) of the shot.

Dubbing The term applies to different editing procedures. 1. The rerecording of dialogue in a film when only a cue track was running during the original shooting. The technical term is *Electronic Line Replacement* (ELR). See *ADR*. 2. Coordinating and synchronizing into a master track all the dialogue and sound tracks from a finished shoot and integrating that track with the film footage. 3. Recording voices, in a foreign language, that will replace the original dialogue in a film. (Speaking in a foreign language while creating the impression that the speeches are coming from the mouths of the original actors in the film is a highly specialized skill.)

Editing Room See *Cutting Room.*

ELR Abbreviation for Electronic Line Replacement. See *ADR; Dubbing.*

Emmy The achievement award statuette given by the Academy of Television Arts and Sciences (equivalent to the Oscar for feature films).

End Marker (Also called *end slate* and *tail slate*.) The slate photographed at the end of a take if, for some reason, a slate was not photographed at the beginning, or if there was a mistake on the beginning slate. An end slate is held upside-down to be photographed.

End Slate See *End Marker.*

End Titles The list of names acknowledging the participants in a film or television production, shown at the end of the presentation. See *Credits.*

Enters Subjects coming into a shot through a door or coming into the frame from off-camera (OC).

Entrance Subjects make an entrance when they come into a shot. See *Enters.*

Establishing Shot A wide-angle, long, or full shot that is made to introduce a particular locale by showing the geography, environment, or atmosphere of a scene.

Exterior Designation for scenes that take place out of doors.

Extreme Close-up The frame holds only a portion of a face, body, or object; the image is magnified.

Extreme Long Shot The frame holds subjects or objects that appear in the distant background of a shot.

Fade In 1. The process whereby a clear image emerges onto the screen from blackness. The process is executed at an optical laboratory. 2. In a script, the term is customarily used to indicate the start of a screenplay or teleplay, and/or the start of a new sequence.

Fade Out 1. The reverse of *Fade In:* the image on the screen disappears into blackness. The process is executed at an optical laboratory. 2. In a script, the term is customarily used to indicate the end of a screenplay or teleplay, and/or the end of a sequence.

Fast Motion Action seen moving at a faster-than-normal pace. The effect is created by undercranking the camera speed (i.e., rolling at less than 24 frames per second [fps]).

Favor The term used to indicate that a character or an object is to be given a position of prominence in a shot.

Field of View See *Angle.*

Final Cut The ultimate edit of a finished film.

First Team Refers to the principal performers in a scene to differentiate them from the stand-ins who were in the set during the lighting.

Flashback Scenes that relate to something in the past, interjected (intercut) between scenes of the contemporary exposition of the story.

Flash Pan The camera moves very swiftly from one image to another, blurring the former and focusing on the latter.

Flopped Film A reversed piece of film. Sometimes a shot is reversed during editing to correct its screen direction. This does not always work, however, particularly when the background is recognizable and numbers and objects are seen backward.

Flub The term for an inadvertent error in dialogue or action made by a performer.

Focal Length   The distance between the optical center of a lens and the subject being filmed. The size of the lens determines the size of the image.

Focus   The point at which a lens produces a sharp image.

Foley   The technique of augmenting and creating sound effects to synchronize with the action in a film during post-production (e.g., footsteps, slaps, punches, heavy breathing). Foley is the surname of the man who invented this technique.

Follow Focus   The adjustment of lens sizes, made according to the changes in distances as a subject, or the camera, moves within a shot. The operation is handled by the Camera First Assistant.

Foreground   1. The space that is closest to the camera. 2. Any area or activity that is in front of the subjects or objects being filmed.

fps (frames per second)   Relates to the measurement of motion picture film. The 35mm camera runs at the speed of 24 fps; it exposes 16 frames per foot, which translates to 1½ feet of film per second, or 90 feet of film per minute. The 16mm camera running at 24 fps exposes 40 frames per foot, which translates to 3/5 of a foot of film per second, or 36 feet of film per minute.

Frame   An individual measure of motion picture film on which an image is projected.

Framing/To Frame   The act of positioning the camera and adjusting the lens to achieve the desired dimension of the subject or area being filmed, sometimes called *lining up.*

Freeze Frame   The holding of an image on a single frame of film that runs as long as required. This gives the impression of suddenly stopped action.

From the Top   An expression that mandates the repeating of a scene from its starting point or from the first word of an actor's speech.

Full Shot   The frame holds subjects from head to toe and the screen is filled with some foreground and/or background activity (see *Long Shot*).

Full Three Shot (F3/SH)   The frame holds three subjects in full figure.

Full Two Shot (F2/SH)   The frame holds two subjects in full figure.

Gobo   A piece of black wood or opaque fabric mounted on a stand, used to prevent rays of light from hitting the camera lens. Gobos come in various shapes and sizes.

Group Shot   The frame holds four or more subjects. The projected image may be in a long shot, a medium shot, or a close shot. The size of the lens determines the size of the image.

Hand-Held Camera   See *Arriflex; Steadicam.*

Head-On Shot   A shot in which the action advances directly toward the camera.

High Angle   The camera is shooting from a height, focusing downward on a scene. See *Boom Camera; Crane Shot.*

High Hat/Hi Hat   A very low tripod on which a camera head is mounted for shooting scenes from below eye level. Sometimes the equipment is placed in a dugout in the ground to achieve the desired filmic effect. The device acquired its name because it resembles a man's evening top hat.

HMI (Halogen Medium Iodide)   A high-intensity, lightweight lamp whose rays simulate daylight brightness. See *Arc Light; Brute.*

"Hold That One"   A director's instruction to the continuity supervisor and the camera assistant not to circle a particular take number for printing but to mark it as a "hold" until further notice.

Honey Wagon   A trailer equipped with washroom facilities, put into service when companies shoot at outdoor locations.

Hubba-hubba   The murmuring sounds emanating from a crowd in a scene, on instruction from the AD.

IATSE   Abbreviation for International Alliance of Theatrical and Stage Employees—the trade union that embraces all the personnel working in film and television production.

Idiot Cards   See *Cue Cards.*

Insert   1. A separate close-up shot that focuses attention on an object within the context of a scene (e.g., a letter, a picture, the time on a clock, a book title, a diamond ring on a finger or in an open box). 2. A shot used as a cutaway during editing.

Insert Car   An automobile, truck, or improvised vehicle in which the camera and select personnel ride when filming a scene that depicts a traveling vehicle.

In Sync   Denotes that camera film and sound track are running at coordinated speed.

Intercut   See *Cross Cutting.*

Interior   Designation for scenes that take place indoors.

IPS (Inches Per Second)   The measurement of sound track (audio tape). Tape runs at the speed of 7½ inches per second. That rate corresponds to the camera's rate of speed of 24 frames per second (fps). When camera and sound record simultaneously at those rates of speed, they are synchronized (*in sync*).

Iris In   The effect of making an image emerge from a speck of light on a black screen (a tiny aperture in the camera) to a fully lit picture. The process is executed at an optical laboratory.

Iris Out   The opposite of *Iris In.* A fully lit picture is gradually diminished until the screen is in total blackness. The process is executed at an optical laboratory.

Juicer   An electrician who connects electrical currents (juice) to lamps and equipment.

Key Light   The principal source of light that illuminates a subject in the set, around which auxiliary lamps are affixed to create the desired ambience of the set.

128

Left-to-Right A camera direction that denotes movement from the left side to the right side of the screen.

Lens An optical device in the camera, through which light passes and projects an image onto film.

Level The relative degree of sound transmitted to the recording panel.

Lining Up See *Framing*.

Lip Sync The technique of synchronizing voice with filmed lip movements in order to replace faulty sound track in scenes shot previously. The procedure takes place in a dubbing room, where the picture is projected on a screen. The actors, wearing earphones, listen as they watch themselves in the film. They then speak the dialogue at the same pace and with the same inflection as in the original performance. The dialogue is recorded impeccably, and the sound track of the *dubbed* voices then supersedes the original *cue tracks* when the final footage is edited. If actors are not adept at lip-syncing, the audience becomes aware of the mechanical contrivance. Sometimes the editor may have to resort to the tactic of cutting away from the on-camera character and laying in the sound track of the clear dialogue over another character's face.

Live Feed A live video performance projected on a television screen within a scene being filmed with a motion-picture camera.

Long Shot A shot of subjects or objects that are distant from the camera, embracing a comprehensive view of the scene (see *Full Shot*). The images in long shots look small to the audience.

Loop The device for running film during lip-syncing recordings.

Looping See *Dubbing*.

Loose Shot A shot in which the frame holds subjects and objects with space at both sides of the image, as opposed to a *tight shot,* wherein the image fills the frame from side to side.

Low Angle See *Angle; High Hat*.

Master Shot The film that comprises the continuous performance of a scene, which includes dialogue and camera moves. Any portion of a scene, or any subject matter related to a scene, that is being filmed for the first time is in the category of *master shot*.

Match Cut In editing, the technique of cutting film when characters are in movement. This achieves the semblance of continuous action between two joined pieces of film that have been shot separately.

Medium Close-up The frame holds the subjects' figures from the waist up, filling the frame at either side.

Medium Close Shot Same as *Medium Close-up,* but with space (air) surrounding the figures.

Medium Long Shot The frame holds the figures from the ankles or calves up, and also holds activity in front of and behind the principal action.

Medium Shot The frame holds the subjects' figures from the thighs up and surrounded by space (air); also referred to as a *loose shot*.

Mirror Shot A shot of a subject's reflection in a mirror. Care must be taken to ensure that no incongruous room reflections intrude.

Mismatch An error in continuity caused by action that was not performed consistently in two consecutive shots within the same scene: action that was filmed from two different angles (e.g., a cut from a full shot to a close shot, or vice versa).

Mock-up 1. A replica made of a structure or an object featured in a scene, particularly when the script calls for its destruction (e.g., a building that burns). 2. A replica made of a section of an automobile, airplane, theatre, or the like, for the purpose of shooting close-up angles for the dialogue or reactions of the characters occupying the seats.

Montage A filmic effect used to convey a story point: a series of shots (cuts or dissolves) that indicate a passage of time or a dramatic succession of events.

MOS The shooting of film without recording sound (silent).

Moviola The trade name for the machine that the editor uses to view film. See *Cutting Room.*

Moving Shot Denotes that the subjects or objects being filmed are in movement, and the camera physically follows them.

NABET The abbreviation for the National Alliance of Broadcast Engineers and Technicians. This organization has expanded to include the motion picture craftspeople in independent production and is an alternative labor organization to IATSE.

Nagra The brand name for a portable tape recorder.

NG The initials for "No Good," applied to anything that is unacceptable for any reason.

Night-for-Day Denotes the filming of outdoor scenes that take place in the daytime but are filmed at night to expedite the schedule. The sets are illuminated by special lamps that emit rays that simulate daylight. See *Arc Light; HMI.*

Night-for-Night Denotes the nighttime filming of outdoor scenes that take place at night. Also denotes the nighttime filming of indoor night scenes when the set must reveal actual darkness of night when shooting through a door or window.

No Print The comment made by the director to indicate that the last recorded take is not to be printed at the laboratory; it is so marked by the continuity supervisor, the camera assistant, and the sound mixer.

Off-Camera (OC) Refers to an action or sound that is out of the range of camera view.

Off-Mike Refers to a voice or sound that is out of the range of the boom microphone.

Off-Screen (OS) Refers to an action or sound that is within the limits of the shot but out of the range of the camera's view. See *Off-Camera.* (OC and OS are often used interchangeably.)

On a Bell   Refers to the time period after a single bell warns that all stirring within the sound stage or shooting area must cease for the duration of filming a take. When the take is finished, a double bell signals that activity may resume.

On Camera   Refers to subjects or objects that are in front of the camera, being filmed.

Out of Frame   Refers to subjects, objects, or parts thereof that are not within the picture projected by the camera lens.

Out of Sync   Means that the running speeds of the camera and the sound track do not coincide (the sight and sound do not match).

Out Take   1. A shot that was not printed (see *"B" Negative*). 2. A piece of film that was deleted in the course of editing.

Overcrank   To run a camera at a speed of more than the normal 24 fps. This creates *slow motion* on the screen.

Overlap   1. The portion of action that is carried over (repeated) from the end of one shot to the beginning of another shot for editing continuity (see *Match Cut*). 2. What occurs when a voice or any off-camera sound intrudes on the dialogue of on-camera subjects.

Over the Shoulder   A filmic composition wherein the frame holds two subjects, one facing the camera and the other with back to the camera and only one shoulder tipped in at the foreground of the frame, either at camera right or camera left.

Pan/Panning   1. The horizontal movement of the camera head on its axis, from left to right (pan right) or right to left (pan left). 2. A panning shot reveals a *pan*oramic view of a scene. 3. The term also denotes a negative opinion of a theatrical production (a bad review).

Parallel Action   See *Cross Cutting*.

Pickup   The term applies: 1. When an incomplete shot is printed and the continuation of that scene begins at the point where the previous shot ended. 2. When only a portion of a shot is repeated to correct a flaw. 3. When a significant change is desired in a portion of the dialogue or action after a shot has been printed.

Picture Time   The actual number of minutes and seconds of picture footage that remain after the final editing of a film.

Platform   A panel of plywood or other material, placed over an area of ground or stage floor that is uneven. This device makes it possible for the wheels of a camera dolly to roll smoothly during shooting.

Playback   The prerecorded singing and/or music played during the filming of musical productions.

POV (Point of View)   A scene shot from the viewpoint of a character in a filmed scene. It reveals to the audience what the character sees.

Production Board   A contrivance devised and used by the AD. It consists of a number of strips of colored cardboard that contain information on all the essential elements for the film and that are arranged in the order of shooting. This device helps the AD to expedite the shooting schedule on a day-by-day basis.

Protection Shot   See *Cover Shot.*

Pull Back   See *Dolly Back.*

Push In   See *Dolly In.*

Rake Shot   The frame holds subjects or objects positioned in a row. The camera angle is from either screen right or screen left and focuses on the line of profiles, shooting past the character or object closest to the camera.

Raw Stock   Film that has not been exposed.

Retake   A take that was done over (reshot) after it had been processed at the laboratory.

Rig   To install equipment in preparation for shooting a film set.

Right-to-Left   A camera direction that denotes movement from the right side to the left side of the screen.

Riser   See *Apple Box.*

"Roll 'Em"   The order given by the AD to the camera operator and the sound mixer to activate their equipment for the making of a shot.

"Roll Film"   The AD's order to activate the camera without the corresponding sound track.

"Roll Sound"   The AD's order to activate the recorder without the rolling of the camera.

Room Tone   See *Ambient (Atmosphere) Sound Track.*

Rough Cut   The first stage of editing a film, wherein film footage and sound track are assembled in proper continuity but without precise timing or editorial refinements.

Running Time   See *Picture Time.*

Rushes   See *Dailies.*

SAG   Abbreviation for Screen Actors Guild.

SC   Abbreviation for *Scene.*

Scenario   1. Another word for screenplay or teleplay. 2. A synopsis of a script giving essential details of the plot, scenes, and characters.

Scene   A segment of a script that describes the activity within a single time period in a given locale.

Scene Number   The identification applied to a scene within a script.

Scenery   1. The décor of a film set, reflecting an authentic locale or environment. 2. Natural vistas that are pictorialized on film.

Score   The music that accompanies a film. It may be music that was produced independently from the film (public domain) or music written especially for it.

Screen Credit   See *Credits.*

Screen Direction   The indication of movement within a frame of film: right to left, left to right, toward background, toward foreground.

Screen Test   Traditionally, a filmed audition to determine whether an actor suits a particular role in a film. These days, in the interest of economics, screen tests are recorded on videotape.

Screening   The showing of a film to a privileged audience.

Screenplay   Material written in a particularly stylized format that is used in the process of filmmaking.

Scrim   A piece of special gauze mounted on a stand and placed between the camera and the characters being filmed. This diffuses the light and lessens the sharpness of the image, so that subjects' blemishes may be diminished or erased.

Script   Any material written for dramatization. See *Scenario; Screenplay; Teleplay.*

Second Unit   An auxiliary production crew that films scenes in which the principal actors are not featured or are portrayed by substitute performers (*doubles*).

SEG   The abbreviation for Screen Extras Guild.

Sequence   Refers to a segment of a script that depicts a continuance of interrelated scenes or shots. Sometimes the term is used synonymously with *scene.*

Set   The specific site where filming takes place.

Setup   The prescribed area in a set on which the camera and sound are focused for the making of a shot.

Shoot   1. The operation of camera and sound that transfers a performance or a setting onto film. 2. The whole process of filming a script ("What's the schedule for this shoot?").

Shooting   The operation of the camera in filming performances or scenery or both. The term applies also to the operation of sound equipment.

Shooting Schedule   The form, prepared by the AD, that lists all the pertinent information extracted from the production board for use by all the production personnel. The schedule details all the elements of who, what, where, and when, together with the number of scenes and pages to be shot each working day for the length of time it takes to complete the filming of the project.

Shooting Script   The script, after all revisions of action and dialogue have been finalized and the pages put into acceptable form to proceed with the shooting of the film.

Short Ends   The raw stock (unexposed film) that remains at the tail end of a magazine of film. These pieces of film proved too short for use in making another take.

Shot   Describes an image that has been satisfactorily recorded by the camera on a continuous length of film (with or without sound). The term applies to the gamut of angles and perspectives that are fashioned by the camera: Long Shot, Medium Shot, Close-up, High or Low Angle, etc.

Shot List   The director's prepared memorandum enumerating the shots and camera angles envisioned to cover the action described in the script.

Silent   See *MOS*.

Single   A shot in which the frame holds only one subject, the angle being either a full shot, a medium shot, or a close shot.

Slate   The small blackboard (also called *clapboard*) that is photographed at the start of every take. It serves to identify the shot numbers of film and sound required by the editor and the laboratory.

Soft Focus   A focus used so that an image is not sharply defined on the screen. Sometimes soft-focus shots are made for filmic effect.

Sound Effects (SFX)   1. Sounds that are indicated in the script but not recorded during shooting. These sounds are recorded subsequently and included in the final editing of the film. 2. The audio components in a film that are made to imitate real sounds. See *Foley*.

Sound Stage   The soundproof studio in which the shooting of film and sound takes place.

Sound Track   1. A length of film carrying sound only. 2. The portion of motion-picture film that is reserved for sound. One or more bands of sound, such as stereophonic recordings, are channeled along one side of the film and thus embody the audio component of the film. The process is executed in a laboratory.

Special Effects (SPFX)   The illusions that are seen on the screen, which have been created by special-effects personnel with the help of mechanical devices. Special effects include visual simulations of fires, explosions, lightning, rain, and supernatural creatures.

Speed   The term used by the sound mixer to announce that the speed of the recorder is synchronized with the speed of the camera.

Splice   In editing, to join together two pieces of cut film.

Split Screen   Two or more separate scenes projected onto one frame of film.

Steadicam   The trade name for a contemporary hand-held camera. It affords greater mobility and steadiness in shooting because it is firmly affixed to the body of the operator. See *Arriflex*.

Stock Shot   A length of film obtained from a film library.

Storyboard   A pictorial layout of scenes or shots for a film, rendered by an artist, to help the director visualize written descriptions in a script. In special-effects films, the storyboard is an essential part of the operation.

Straight Cut   In continuity editing, two shots joined directly to each other without any optical effect between them.

Subjective Pan   The camera moves slowly and methodically across a scene, creating the sense that eyes are scanning the tableau. The technique is used to evoke suspense, shock, surprise, or a sense of danger.

Subtitles   The printed words, superimposed on the lower part of a screen, that are translations of a foreign language.

Superimposure   The process of placing one image on top of another without obliterating the first image. The filmic technique of superimposing an image on an actor's face to depict what the actor is subliminally visualizing is known as *stream of consciousness*. The effect is a transparent double image that lets the audience see what the actor is thinking. The subject of the mental picture is written into the script as a separate scene number, with the notation "To Be Superimposed."

Swish Pan   See *Flash Pan.*

Sync   Short for *synchronization* or *synchronized.* See *In Sync; IPS; Out of Sync.*

Tag   A brief scene that marks the finish of a film. It ties up the loose ends of the story. Such scenes are most prevalent in films for television.

Tail Slate   See *End Marker.*

Take   An image that has been recorded on film (with or without sound).

Teaser   A brief, enticing scene or a series of intriguing shots at the start of a television film, intended to capture the audience's attention.

Teleplay   A script written especially for a television production. See *Screenplay.*

"That's a Hold"   See *Hold That One.*

The Trades   The industry's periodicals, particularly *Daily Hollywood Reporter, Daily Variety, and Dramalogue.* There are several others.

Tight Shot   A shot in which the frame holds subjects or objects that fill the space to the left and right sides of the screen.

Tilting   The vertical movement of the camera head on its axis as it pans upward and downward (see *Pan/Panning*). The tilting of the camera head produces a movement that is distinct from the vertical movement of the boom camera (see *Boom Camera*).

Titles   The name and any inscription that appear at the beginning or end of a film or television presentation (known as *opening* and *closing titles*).

Tracking Shot   A shot made when the camera is mounted on a dolly and moved on tracks to follow actors as they walk or run. See *Dolly Tracks.*

Traveling Shot   A shot in which the camera is filming a traveling vehicle (see *Insert Car*). Another modus operandi is to mount one or two cameras on the principal vehicle—attached to the outside of the doors or the hood—and film the passengers riding in the car.

Treatment   A written synopsis of a story, delineating the main scenes and some dialogue. A treatment is prepared with the intention of developing it into a screenplay or teleplay.

Tripod   A three-legged adjustable stand on which a camera is affixed.

Trucking Shot   Same as *Tracking Shot.* A script may read, "Camera trucks along with John and Mary as they walk." Make note of: (a) *Camera Preceding,* to indicate that the camera is focused on the subjects' faces, which are moving toward the camera. (b) *Camera Following,* to indicate that the camera is focused on the subjects' backs, which are moving away from the camera. (c) *Side Angle,* to indicate that the camera is focused on the subjects' profiles, which are moving either left to right or right to left.

Turn-Around Time   The time allowed after a company has been shooting night-for-night so that the actors and craftspeople can get sufficient rest before daytime shooting resumes.

Two Shot (2/SH)   The frame holds two subjects. It may be a full shot, medium shot, or close shot.

Undercrank   To run the camera at a speed of less than the normal 24 fps. This creates fast motion on the screen.

Upstage   The area farthest from the camera. Moving upstage means moving toward the rear (BG) of the setup.

Video   The visual components in film and television.

Viewfinder   1. The optical instrument through which the director of photography (DP) peers to ascertain the depth of field (view) of a setup. 2. A component of the camera through which the operator looks to see how the image will be recorded on film.

Voice Over (VO)   A voice heard on screen without the appearance of the speaker (e.g., narration).

Voice Slate   The announcement of slate and take numbers by *voicing* them into the recording panel when it is inexpedient to simultaneously photograph the corresponding slate.

Walla-Walla   See *Hubba-Hubba*.

Walkie-Talkie   Hand-radio communication between the director, the AD, and the second assistant director when shooting far-spread action.

Whip Pan   See *Flash Pan*.

Wide Angle   A camera angle in which the frame holds a large area, with a crowd of people and/or objects positioned at a distance from the camera. The lens' focal length makes the full figures appear small on the screen. Or the composition may be with the principal players positioned in the center or foreground of the scene, while the shot encompasses the activity behind and at both sides of the principals. The latter composition is described as *shooting past* the principals (from their ankles, knees, or thighs, as the case may be).

Wild Line   A phrase or a word from a speech that needs to be repeated because of poor enunciation in the original shot. Rather than do a retake with film, a wild line is recorded on tape only, to be *laid in* by the editor during editing.

Wiped Out   Describes a sound erased from a tape recorder.

Wipe   A transition from one scene to another. The image on the screen is virtually wiped off as it reveals another image behind it. The process is executed at an optical laboratory.

Wrap   The finish of a sequence or the end of an entire shoot: "That's a wrap."

Zip Pan   See *Flash Pan*.

Zoom In   The same as *Dolly In; Push In;* done with the zoom lens.

Zoom Out   The same as *Dolly Back; Pull Back;* done with the zoom lens.

9

Dynamics of
the Camera

THE EYE OF THE CAMERA

Camera technology is the domain of camera personnel and the director. But it will benefit you to be conversant with some of the terminology and principles governing camera dynamics.

Try to acquire the habit of visualizing a movie set in relation to a frame of film so that you will always think in terms of screen (camera) direction. A set is a three-walled area: there is the left side of the frame, known as *Camera Left* (CL), the right side of the frame, known as *Camera Right* (CR), and the *background* (BG) of the frame. The camera and the audience are the "fourth wall." When shooting interiors, the background limit is a wall or a structure. When shooting exteriors, the background limit is determined by the camera's cutoff point—in other words, the most distant point at which the camera lens can hold the image in clear focus (see *Depth of Field* under "Definitions of Industry Terms" in Chapter 8).

Film is gauged in millimeters: 35mm, 16mm, and 8mm denote the width of the celluloid from which film is manufactured. Most motion-picture photography is shot with 35mm cameras, while documentaries are customarily shot with 16mm cameras, and home movies or student projects are shot with 8mm cameras.

INSCRIBED AREA

What the camera sees (what the frame holds) is referred to as the *inscribed area*. More specifically, the inscribed area is the space that the image takes up within a single frame—from side to side, top to bottom, and in spatial depth—whether the image is in wide angle or close up.

Every movement of the camera, however slight, creates an angle change; every shift of lens size creates an angle change. Each change makes a difference in the inscribed area. As continuity supervisor, your main concern at all times is what the frame is holding in any given angle, and how the image appears in the camera, not how it actually appears to your normal vision. It is your prerogative to peer into the camera to make sure that your shot description is accurate.

IMAGINARY LINE/ACTION AXIS/
180° RULE

The filmic principle that dictates the placement of the camera within a given spatial sphere is referred to as the *imaginary line,* the *action axis,* or the *180° rule.* A stationary camera on a tripod, moving its head left to right or right to left, pans a semicircle of 180°. The circumference of a circle, of course, measures 360°. The camera's viewpoint on any fixed shot predicates the principle of the 180° rule/action axis/imaginary line of that shot.

The concept of the imaginary line can better be delineated as the drawing of a theoretical line extending straight across the scene in the line of eye contact between the two subjects closest to the camera on each side of the frame. The concept mandates that all component shots be confined within the area in front of the imaginary line of the fixed shot. Thus, congruity will be maintained when intercutting the related shots (see Figure 9.1). Adherence to the imaginary line is an UNBREAKABLE LAW. Should a component shot be made with the camera having crossed to the other side of the line, the image on the screen will appear in reverse.

The only time that crossing the line (violating the 180° rule) will not disturb continuity is when the camera follows the subjects' movements within the setup, panning and dollying with the action. So long as the camera and actors are in movement, there is no commitment to the imaginary line. However, should the camera and the actors stop at a given point while the dialogue continues, that stationary angle creates a new imaginary line. And if the director decides to cover (break up) this camera viewpoint with close-ups, then those component shots will have to adhere to the last fixed imaginary line.

CROSSING THE LINE

Example 1

Let us say that a master 2/Shot (Figure 9.1) is covered by two single closer angles. In Shot 1 (Figure 9.2), the camera is focused on Character A looking CR to Character B. In Shot 2 (Figure 9.3), the camera is focused on Character B looking CL to Character A. But if the camera were positioned incorrectly in the latter shot (i.e., if it had *crossed the line*), then Character B, on the screen, would suddenly be looking CR—the opposite direction (see Figure 9.4)—even though the character and the chair remained in exactly the same position as in the master shot. This shot therefore cannot be intercut with either the master 2/Shot or the close-up on Character A.

Figure 9.1

A B

Imaginary line

Figure 9.2

Shot 1

Figure 9.3

Shot 2

Figure 9.4

Shot 2

Camera crossed the line and created a reverse shot. B's look to CR is wrong. This shot cannot be intercut with either the master 2/Shot or A's close-up.

Example 2

Let us say that a vehicle filmed traveling the road left-to-right (Figure 9.5) is also filmed from another location, on the opposite side of the road (Figure 9.6). The vehicle will appear on the screen as though it is suddenly traveling in the opposite direction (right-to-left) instead of traveling progressively in the one direction as originally intended. If these two pieces of film were joined in editing, the screen would show the car in the first shot and the car in the second shot traveling toward each other. In other words, it would appear to the audience that the same vehicle is headed for a collision with itself (see Figures 9.7 and 9.8).

Let me caution: In the course of shooting a film, you will sometimes encounter disputes over this technicality; there are lawbreakers among filmmakers. Your expertise notwithstanding, the final decision rests with the director. All you can do is make a notation in your continuity script to the editor that you mentioned this incongruity to the director.

Car traveling L-R, camera positioned shooting past the passenger.

Camera positioned on opposite side of the road, now shooting past the driver, makes the car travel R-L (reverse direction). Turn page upside-down to seen direction from the point of view of this camera.

Figure 9.5

Figure 9.6

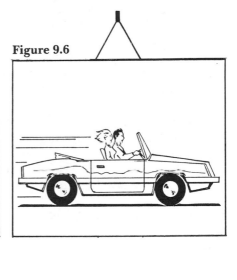

Figure 9.7

Figure 9.8

When these two shots are joined in editing, it appears that the one vehicle is headed for a collision with itself.

PROGRESSION

The principle of *camera progression* is the maintaining of an uninterrupted flow of movement in the same direction from one shot to the next. In other words, if it is established at the start of a sequence that subjects (persons, animals, vehicles) will enter a shot camera left (CL) and exit the shot camera right (CR), or enter a shot camera right (CR) and exit the shot camera left (CL), then all succeeding shots connected to that sequence must follow the same progression until the action stops at a predetermined destination.

No matter how far apart the locations of the related shots may be, or how differently the sets are designed—high angle, low angle, or side angle—the established progression continuity must be maintained throughout.

Cinematically, the technique conveys natural progression to the audience. Like the 180° rule, the law of progression cannot be broken. If the rule is violated in any one of the succession of shots in a sequence, the result is a confusing picture of subjects moving in opposite directions. The audience becomes disconcerted when progression shots are not consistent.

Clean Entrances and Exits

It is mandatory that subjects make a *clean entrance* (from outside the frame) into every shot and a *clean exit* (to outside the frame) from every shot. The editor cannot preserve the flow of progression if a supposedly moving subject does not completely clear the frame at the end of a shot or is in a still position in the frame at the start of a following shot. Experienced camera operators are cognizant of this principle and will not switch the camera off before the subjects have cleared the frame (see Figure 9.9).

Figure 9.9

PROGRESSION:
Clean Entrances and Exits

Right-to-Left

Location #1

Left-to-Right

Location #1

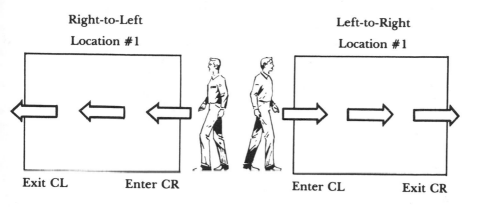

Exit CL   Enter CR   Enter CL   Exit CR

Location #2   **Location #2**

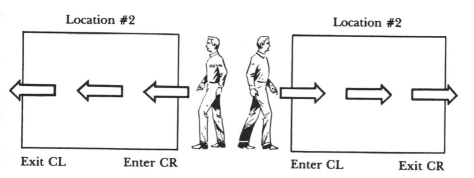

Exit CL   Enter CR   Enter CL   Exit CR

Location #3   **Location #3**

Enter frame at CR,
stop at destination   Enter frame at CL,
stop at destination

The Chasing Action

When two characters are moving in the same direction—say, left-to-right (stalking or chasing each other)—each character must make a clean entrance into every shot and a clean exit out of every shot at the same pace as in the previous shot. This progression must be strictly observed, no matter how far apart the individual location sites may be or how much time elapses between shooting the number of setups called for in the sequence.

Also, since the locations involved in a chase sequence are often not shot in the rotations depicted in the script, no segment of the chase may deviate from the established progression (see Figure 9.10). You must be unerring in your progression continuity.

Figure 9.10

PROGRESSION:
The Chasing Action

Location #1

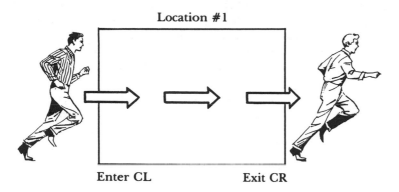

Enter CL   Exit CR

Location #2

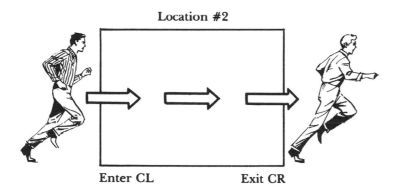

Enter CL   Exit CR

Location #3

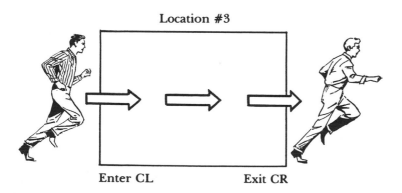

Enter CL   Exit CR

The Converging Action

The same strict fidelity to progression applies when characters or vehicles are supposed to be moving toward each other. The progression will be as follows: one will move left-to-right (L–R) and the other will move right-to-left (R–L). In every setup, each subject will make clean entrances and clean exits. At a point in the story when the subjects are supposed to come together, each will make the proper entrance from opposite sides of the camera into the same frame—and meet (see Figure 9.11).

It all comes together in the editing room. The editor will assemble all the pieces in their appropriate order, according to the director's instructions, and the result on the screen will be an engrossing, continuous episode.

Figure 9.11

PROGRESSION:
The Converging Action

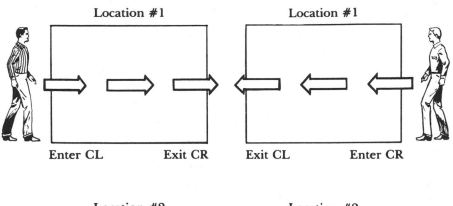

Location #1	Location #1
Enter CL Exit CR	Exit CL Enter CR

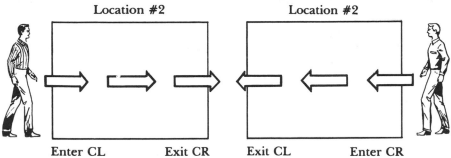

Location #2	Location #2
Enter CL Exit CR	Exit CL Enter CR

Location #3

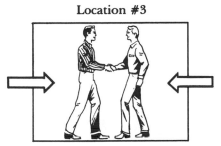

At destination, two characters
enter frame from each side of
camera and meet

Direct Reverse Progression

There are times when proper progression is maintained although the camera is placed in a reverse position. For example, a couple enters a large room where a party is in progress; in the background is a table with punch bowl and glasses. The camera is focused on the couple's backs (Figure 9.12) as they walk toward the background table (away from camera). At a certain point in their walk, the shot will be cut, either (1) because the director wants to reveal the couple's identity to the audience, or (2) to shorten the length of the walk for timing purposes. At this point another setup will be made, placing the camera in reverse position (action axis; crossing the line). The camera is now angled toward the door—which is now in the background—shooting past the table in the foreground and holding on the faces of the couple (Figure 9.13).

NOTE: This reverse angle will change the couple's positions on the screen: in the first shot, the man is on CL and the woman is on CR; in the reverse shot, the man is on CR and the woman is on CL. As the couple continues their walk (moving toward camera) to the table in the foreground, the illusion of uninterrupted action is cinematically achieved. For the audience, this reverse technique maintains normal progression within the scene.

Figure 9.12

Figure 9.13

Establishing Geography

When designing sets for a film production, the art director provides a blueprint for the director and the cinematographer that depicts the various set locales in relation to each other from a key point of view of the camera. For instance, in a "town" set, the bank is to the left of the store and to the right of the church; the farmhouse is to the right of the church and to the left of the school (see Figure 9.14). Once this geography is established, the screen direction—from left-to-right and right-to-left, for all the entrances to and exits from these sites—must conform in every shot. There can be no deviation. The audience becomes oriented and identifies with the characters' comings and goings to and from the various locales. When the rules of screen direction are strictly adhered to, it does not matter how disjointedly (out of continuity) the scenes have been shot; ultimately, the film editor will have all the sequences flowing in flawless continuity.

Doubtful Progression

Occasionally, a problem may arise: there is uncertainty as to the shooting progression of a scene from one setup to another. Did the character exit the previous shot camera right (CR) or camera left (CL)? Another problem may arise when proper entrance into a setup cannot be made because of crowded space. The following technique has been developed to overcome these predicaments:

1. Start close-up on the back of a subject—blocking (filling) the screen to create a momentary distraction. As the subject starts to move *away from the camera,* another setup (different scene) is revealed. The subject may then proceed toward CL or CR as required for the scene's progression.
2. Reversing the above, start close-up on the front of a subject's torso— blocking (filling) the screen to create a momentary distraction. As the camera pulls back (dollies back or zooms out) to a wider angle (medium or full shot), another setup (different scene) is revealed. The subject can then move forward (*toward the camera*) to either CL or CR as required for the scene's progression.

Cross-Country Progression

The progression for cross-country travel customarily conforms to the design of the United States map: west is CL, east is CR. You are traveling left-to-right (L–R) when going from Los Angeles to Chicago or New York, and you are traveling right-to-left (R–L) when going from New York to Chicago or Los Angeles.

153

Figure 9.14

Eyes-Following Progression

The geographical position of the camera that is shooting a parade or a moving vehicle determines the way viewers' eyes will follow the moving subjects. For instance, let's say the camera is photographing a parade or a procession along a street, marching right-to-left (R–L). If the people watching are positioned behind the camera (unseen), then the camera will later make another shot in reverse position and photograph the people at the curb viewing the parade. Their eyes will move left-to-right (L–R), the reverse of the parade movement. To achieve the correct looks from the watchers, it is customary to have someone behind the camera hold up a flag and move in the same direction and at the same pace as the parade. When the two pieces of film are intercut, it will appear to the audience that the people are viewing the parade in proper perspective.

SCREEN DIRECTION

The term *screen direction* (also called *camera direction*) refers to the movement of subjects within a frame as they move from side to side (left-to-right [L–R] and right-to-left [R–L]), toward the background (*away from camera*), or toward the foreground (*toward camera*).

When writing shot descriptions, always note the subject's movements in terms of screen direction, i.e., move left-to-right (L–R) or right-to-left (R–L). Also, indicate characters' entrances into and out of a shot (i.e., ENT. CR or CL; X'T CR or CL). If a character comes head on toward the camera and exits the shot, I describe it as X'T *past* CR or CL.

Entering from Off-Camera

Figure 9.15 depicts a hypothetical scene to demonstrate movement within a master shot that holds six people seated at a table. During the playing of the scene, each character will rise and move in the direction indicated in the figure. Having moved within the master shot, the characters must then make entrances into their respective closer angles without creating directional mismatches or jump cuts. The notations indicate the side of the camera from which each character must enter the next setup in order to preserve the illusion of continuous movement from shot to shot.

Figure 9.15

SCREEN DIRECTION
Off-Camera Entrance

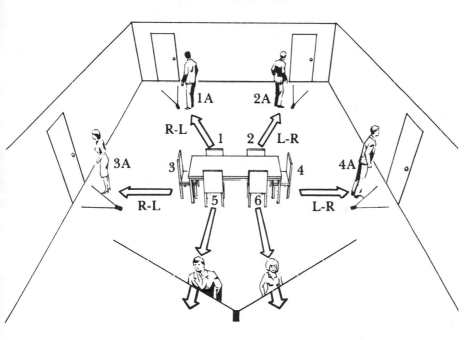

1. Move R–L to Lbg door.
2. Move L–R to Rbg door.
3. Move X-Room R–L to center door.
4. Move X-Room L–R to center door.
5. Move R–L to fg, exit past CL.
6. Move L–R to fg, exit past CR.

1A. Closer Angle on Lbg door; enter from behind CR.

2A. Closer Angle on Rbg door; enter from behind CL.

3A. Closer Angle on center door; enter from behind CR.

4A. Closer Angle on center door; enter from behind CL.

Going through a Door

In order to maintain the filmic illusion of consistent progression in bringing subjects through a door, the compatible positioning of the camera on both sides of the doorway is mandatory (see Figure 9.16).

Shot 1, Exterior (Frame 1): the character is walking left-to-right (L–R) toward the door. Upon reaching the door, the shot will be cut. But the very next shot will be continuous movement *screenwise,* showing the character coming through the door and continuing into the house.

Shot 2, Interior (Frame 2): the camera is positioned on the correct side of the door. When the door is opened, the only direction from which the character can enter the shot is from camera left-to-right (L–R). Thus, continuous progression into the room is maintained.

Shot 2, Interior (Frame 3): the camera is positioned incorrectly, at the other side of the door (see broken lines). On the screen, the character will appear in the middle of the doorway, walking in reverse direction—camera right-to-left (R–L). There is no way that the shots in Frames 1 and 3 can be spliced.

NOTE: Here's a hint for ensuring correct progression for going through a door. When shooting the first scene, make a note (or a diagram) indicating where the doorknob is: either on CR or CL. When shooting the second scene, make sure that the doorknob is on the direct reverse side of the door. If in shot 1, the doorknob was on CR, then in shot 2 it must be on CL (study Figure 9.16).

Frames 1 and 2 can be spliced and the transition can be enhanced by another filmic convention: end the exterior shot (Frame 1) with the opening of the door and make a clean exit from the shot into the interior. Then begin the interior shot (Frame 2) with an overlap of the door being opened from the exterior. In that way, the director gives the editor leeway to effect the smoothest transition.

An exterior scene may well be filmed at an actual outdoor location, while the corresponding interior scene may be built and filmed on a sound stage. There may be a lapse of days, weeks, or even months between the filming of the individual scenes. Whether the exterior or interior scene is filmed first, be sure to note the screen direction of the initial shot and keep a keen eye on how the door is hinged for the second shot.

The technique of maintaining consistent progression applies equally when going through interior doors from room to room.

Figure 9.16

SCREEN DIRECTION
Going through a Door

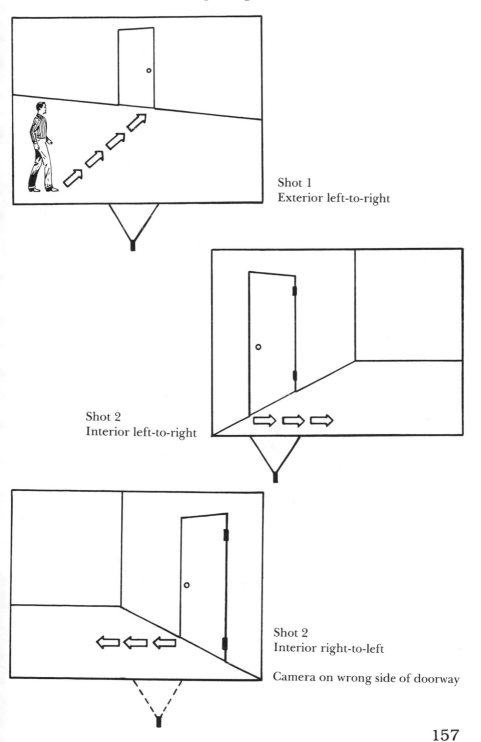

Shot 1
Exterior left-to-right

Shot 2
Interior left-to-right

Shot 2
Interior right-to-left

Camera on wrong side of doorway

158

JUMPS ON SCREEN

When props within a shot are incongruously juxtaposed from one angle to another, *jumps* occur on the screen. Figure 9.17 depicts a couple seated at either side of a table with a candle placed in the center. If the master 2/shot is to be covered by two single close angles, it must be determined beforehand "who gets the candle?" It is a cinematic dictum that the prop cannot appear in both close shots. If the candle is included in both shots, here's what will happen: when cross-cutting the dialogue between the man and the woman, the candle will appear to *jump* from one side of the screen to the other, from camera right (see Close shot A) to camera left (see Close shot B). The audience's eyes will gravitate to the glaring juxtaposition of the candle on the table, and their attention will be diverted from the couple's important dialogue. Such filmic distractions dissipate the dramatics of a scene.

Figure 9.17

Master 2/Shot

Close shot—A

Candle on CR

Close shot—B

Candle on CL

HAND-HELD CAMERA

The *hand-held camera* is just what the term implies. Instead of being mounted on a tripod (stationary) or on dolly wheels (moving), the camera is portable—held on the shoulders of a camera person. The trade name of this camera is *Arriflex;* it is sometimes referred to as the *Arri.*

The mobility of the Arri camera enables the camera technician to achieve special photographic effects, such as swish pans, images on a slant, or provocative distorted shots. The hand-held camera is used effectively when it circulates in a crowd to capture spontaneous reactions and extreme close-ups. Hand-held shots often dynamically punctuate the principal photography.

In recent years, advances have been made in hand-held cameras. They are now equipped with special gear to ensure greater body balance for the camera operator and greater camera steadiness for filming. One such apparatus is the *Steadicam,* which permits filming in tighter areas and effects extraordinary moves that cannot be achieved with conventional dolly-camera equipment. Hand-held cameras also have zoom-lens capabilities. On the down side for this equipment is its poorer film quality.

SPLIT SCREEN

The *split screen* is a trick shot that projects more than one image in a single frame. This is achieved by shooting into only a portion of the frame at a time. The frame is divided into separate panels—vertical, horizontal, or diagonal—and a scene is filmed within one panel while the other portions of the frame are *blocked off* (also called *masked off*). During the filming of each individual panel, the split-screen camera must be immobilized. You will hear the term *tied off,* which means that the camera focus is fixed on one panel. There can be absolutely no movement in the vicinity of the camera; any untoward jar to the camera will create a wavy image on the screen.

Split-screen technique is used when actors play dual roles or when the director wishes to effect a composite of different scenes in one frame.

REAR PROJECTION/PROCESS SHOTS

The technique whereby live action takes place in front of a scene projected on a background screen is called a *rear projection* or *process shot.* For instance, a script calls for a scene played in front of the Empire State Building in New York City. For practical and economic reasons, the actors do not travel to New York City. Instead, they enact the scene on a studio sound stage rigged with rear-projection equipment. The scene of the Empire State

Building and the activity there is projected on a large translucent screen, called a *plate,* while the actors perform the scene in front of it. The rolling of the camera and the rear projector are perfectly synchronized.

Skillfully executed process shots defy detection. The technique has necessarily been practiced prudently because the rigging of the sound stage for rear-projection shooting requires elaborate apparatus and time-consuming lighting maneuvers. This unique practice has largely been superseded by the present-day method of filming at actual locations all around the globe. In the field of special effects, however, process shots are used extensively.

NOTE: Every process plate bears a number. You must announce each plate number with each slate number and mark your continuity script accordingly.

LENSES

The lens is an optical device on the camera. It has an opening (*aperture*) through which light passes and projects an image onto film. The management of lenses is entirely within the camera personnel's scope of operation. Nevertheless, it is to your advantage to be somewhat familiar with a few basic terms pertaining to lens technology.

Focal Length is the gauge of a lens pertaining to the distance between the optical center of the lens in the camera and the subject being filmed. The distance is referred to as the shot's *field of view.* Lenses come in a variety of *focal lengths,* which are measured in millimeters. The standard equivalents are as follows:

25mm = 1 inch
50mm = 2 inches
75mm = 3 inches
100mm = 4 inches

There are also sequentially numbered lenses gauged below, between, and beyond the numbers mentioned above. The lens size determines the size of the image that is projected on the film. Technically, though, the size of the image is also predicated on the placement of the camera. For example, a 100mm lens on a camera positioned a substantial distance from the subject may project an image approximately the same size as that projected by a 75mm lens in a camera positioned closer to the subject.

NOTE: You will find it advantageous to record the lens size in your shot descriptions, together with the measurement between the camera and the subject.

Focus is the point at which a lens produces a sharp image.

Focusing is the act of making a precise lens adjustment to ensure the optimal sharpness of the image. *In focus* means that the projected image is sharply defined. *Out of focus* means that the projected image is not sharply defined.

Depth of Field is the space (distance) between the subject and the camera lens, in which the image is held in sharp focus.

The lower the lens number (i.e., the shorter the focal length), the longer the depth of field. Low-numbered lenses are used for shots that encompass a large area of the scene. In such shots (referred to as *Wide Angles, Full shots, Long shots,* and *Extreme Long shots*), the images projected on the screen look small to the audience because the subjects are seen from a distant perspective.

The higher the lens number (i.e., the longer the focal length), the shorter the depth of field. High-numbered lenses project a larger image on the film, thus bringing the subjects closer to the eyes of the audience. Such shots are referred to as *Medium shots, Close shots,* and *Close-ups.*

Follow Focus means to adjust the lens for changes in distances as subjects move away from or toward the camera, or when the camera moves to follow the action. The camera first assistant (sometimes called the *focus puller*) attends to the camera when such shots are executed. If focus is not followed to maintain depth of field while one subject is in the foreground of the shot and the other is in the background, the subject in the background may look fuzzy because it is in *soft focus.* At times, such images are composed intentionally for filmic effect.

When both the background and foreground images are sharply defined, the shot is referred to as having *split focus.*

F-Stop is a geometric measurement denoting the size of the opening (*aperture*) of the lens, through which the light passes and fixes the sharpness of the picture. The lower the F-number, the less light is required for shooting; the higher the F-number, the more light is required for shooting.

T-Stop refers to the matching of transmitted light from shot to shot.

Zoom Lens is a lens designed with variable focal lengths, which gives the camera the capability of attaining different perspectives and image sizes with the simple twist of a lever while the camera is rolling. With the traditional fixed lens in the camera it is necessary to stop the filming and manually affix a different focal-length lens every time the distance changes between the camera and the subject.

Telephoto Lens is one that can focus on an image from a great distance.

10

Techniques of Coverage

THEORY OF COVERAGE

As mentioned in Chapter 1, scene *coverage* means the *breaking up* of a filmed master shot into a variety of camera angles and closer shots. The principle of coverage is predicated on the theory, evolved by early filmmakers, that punctuating a master wide-angle shot with closer angles and different camera viewpoints heightens the impact of a filmed performance. That conclusion, however, presented another challenge: how to match the action from one piece of film to another after the film of the master shot had been severed. So the precept of coverage became contingent on effective techniques for action-matching. Inasmuch as both elements have to be dealt with simultaneously, I shall, in the interest of clarity, outline the matching techniques in the next chapter.

Coverage is the director's domain, while action-matching comes within the purview of the continuity supervisor.

THE PURPOSE OF COVERAGE

The objective in breaking up a continuous master shot is to emphasize some dramatic or significant aspect in the scene. Another reason for breaking up a master shot is to improve the tempo of a slow-moving performance. By punctuating the action with different angles and close-ups, the pace of the scene can be accelerated. And there are other philosophical reasons: close shots evoke a more intimate relationship between the screen character and the audience; a shot of another character's reaction to a speech or a piece of business brings another dimension to the scene; a big close-up of a menacing weapon held by, or aimed at, the heroine builds tension and suspense.

SHOT SIZES

Figure 10.1 is an overview of shot sizes. The designated terms and their abbreviations are more or less standard.

Figure 10.1

OVERVIEW OF SHOT SIZES

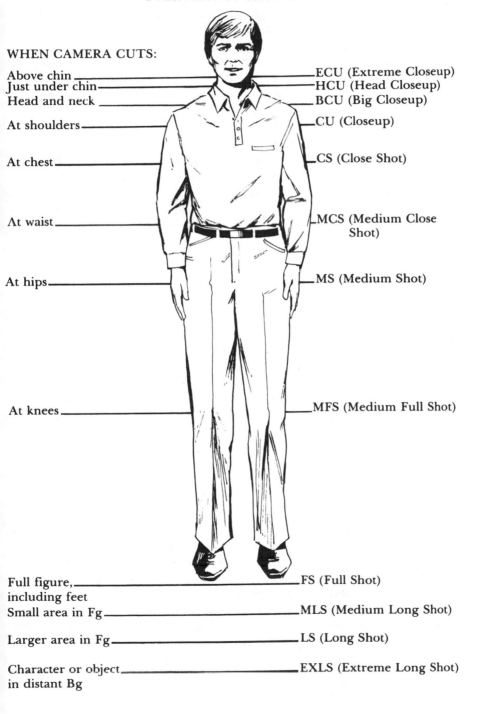

WHEN CAMERA CUTS:

Above chin — ECU (Extreme Closeup)
Just under chin — HCU (Head Closeup)
Head and neck — BCU (Big Closeup)

At shoulders — CU (Closeup)

At chest — CS (Close Shot)

At waist — MCS (Medium Close Shot)

At hips — MS (Medium Shot)

At knees — MFS (Medium Full Shot)

Full figure, including feet — FS (Full Shot)
Small area in Fg — MLS (Medium Long Shot)

Larger area in Fg — LS (Long Shot)

Character or object in distant Bg — EXLS (Extreme Long Shot)

COVERING MASTER SCENES

The master scene has to be designed so that coverage can be achieved without incurring technical snags, such as jump cuts and directional mismatches. When coverage is accomplished smoothly, the editor is able to intercut all the component shots into a continuous, even-flowing sequence. Obviously, a speech or an action can be heard or seen only once in the final cut of the picture. Nonetheless, copious coverage affords the director and the editor creative options for utilizing the most dynamic shots and thus realizing the scene's dramatic potential.

The gamut of coverage depends on the virtuosity of the director. This skill, however, is sometimes throttled by such mundane restrictions as the size of the budget and the schedule of production time. The tighter the budget and the tighter the schedule, the less fancy and varied are the time-consuming setups for coverage.

Figures 10.2, 10.3, and 10.4 will give you an inkling of the various angles (there are many more) that a director may shoot when breaking up (covering) a master scene.

Correct Looks

Because of an idiosyncracy in cinematic technology, there is an inflexible rule that governs the screen direction of characters' *looks* when covering a shot. Let us envision a scene of two characters engaged in conversation, and then the subsequent filming of a close-up of one of the characters. The rule mandates that the off-camera character be positioned at the appropriate side of the camera. The explanation is this: the camera is now positioned where the facing character stood or sat in the master 2/Shot. That makes the on-camera character's eyes look straight into the camera lens, which creates the impression on the screen that this character is speaking to an audience, not to the other character in the master shot. (Newscasters and lecturers look straight into the camera lens as they address a listening audience.) This filmic eccentricity mandates that looks go to either camera-right (CR) or camera-left (CL).

When more than one off-camera character is involved, all must be positioned alongside the camera in the exact rotation, standing or seated, as in the master shot. The character whose position was farthest from the on-camera character in the master shot is now placed closest to the apex of the camera lens to ensure the *correct looks* from the on-camera character. Otherwise, when intercutting the dialogue or the glances between the characters, their positions in relationship to one another become inconsistent. Observe in particular the positioning of the off-camera characters with regard to looks in Figure 10.2, Frames 7 and 8.

Figure 10.2

BREAKING UP THE MASTER—4 People in Frame

1. Full 4/Shot—head to toe.
2. Med. Tight Group 4/Shot—hip figure.
   Fill screen from side to side.

Frame 1

Frame 2

Frame 3

Frame 4

3. X-Angle Rake Shot from stage left. Profiles of A and B in left frame to full faces on C and D in right frame.
4. X-Angle Rake Shot from stage right. Profiles of C and D in right frame to full faces on A and B in left frame.

BREAKING UP THE MASTER—4 People in Frame (Cont'd)

5. Med. Close 2/Shot: A and B—waist figure. Look off CR to C and D.
6. Med. Close 2/Shot: C and D—waist figure. Look off CL to A and B.

Frame 5

Frame 6

Frame 7

Frame 8

7. Close-up: A. Looks off CR to B, C, D.
8. Close-up: D. Looks off CL to C, B, A.

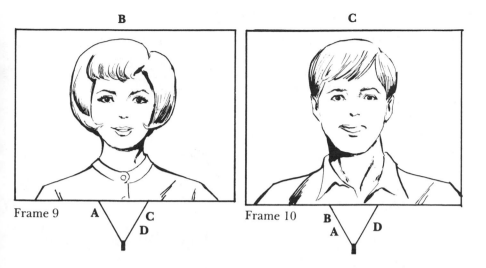

Frame 9   A   C / D

Frame 10   B / A   D

9. Close-up: B (Split Look*). Looks off CL to A. Looks off CR to C and D.

10. Close-up: C (Split Look*). Looks off CL to A and B. Looks off CR to D.

*The Split Look: In Frames 9 and 10, the on-camera characters split their looks to off-camera characters at both CL and CR (in the same setup). For the sake of simplicity, the on-camera characters (B and C) have been drawn to look straight ahead (neutral), leaving it up to the reader to visualize how the heads and eyes will turn to CL and CR as dictated by the dialogue in the scene (see Frame 7, Look CR; and Frame 8, Look CL).

Figure 10.3

BREAKING UP THE MASTER—3 People in Frame

1. Full 3/Shot—head to toe.
2. Med. Tight 3/Shot—waist figure.

Frame 1

Frame 2

Frame 3

Frame 4

3. Close 2/Shot: A and B. Look off CR to C.
   Will intercut with
4. Close-up: C. Looks off CL to B and A.

5. Close-up: A. Looks off CR to B and C.
Will intercut with
6. Close 2/Shot: B and C. Look off CL to A.

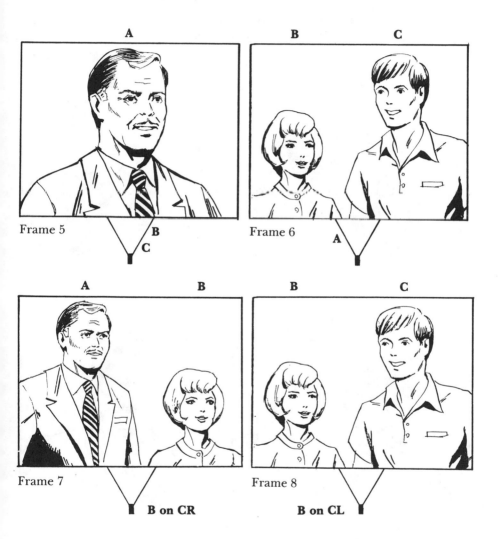

Frame 5 B C

Frame 6 A

Frame 7 **B on CR**

Frame 8 **B on CL**

Frames 7 and 8 are taboo. NEVER break up a 3/Shot into two 2/Shots: center person with person on CL, then center person with person on CR. This will make the center person jump on screen from CR to CL.

Figure 10.4

BREAKING UP THE MASTER—2 People in Frame

1. Full 2/Shot—head to toe.
2. Med. Close 2/Shot—waist figure.

Frame 1   Frame 2

Frame 3   Frame 4

3. Close-up: A. Looks off CR to B.
4. Close-up: B. Looks off CL to A.

5. Over-the-Shoulder Shot: Featuring A looking CR to B. Camera setup is over back of B's *left* shoulder positioned in *right* side of frame.

6. Over-the-Shoulder Shot: Featuring B looking CL to A. Camera setup is over back of A's *right* shoulder positioned in *left* side of frame.

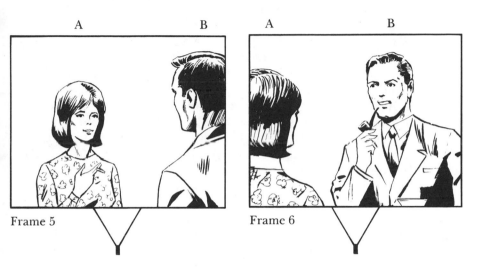

Frame 5   Frame 6

Special information for the over-the-shoulder shots. It is customary to make a companion reverse shot (sometimes referred to as the "answer shot") of the first setup. Always indicate in your shot description which character is facing the camera. In both angles, meticulous care must be taken to match every minute detail that shows in the frame and to position the camera exactly over the correct shoulder. Any inaccuracy makes it impossible to intercut the two angles. Another important detail that requires your close attention is the direction in which the actors turn away from each other or exit at the end of the shot: turn on right or left shoulder. These turns must match their moves in the master 2/shot. Because it makes for smooth continuity editing, editors always like to *cut on movement*.

NOTE: The shooting of the companion reverse angle of an over-the-shoulder shot does not change the relative positions of the characters on the screen, as discussed on page 150 and shown in Figures 9.12 and 9.13.

COVERING WITH DOUBLES

When risk is involved in the performance of a scene—for example, one involving fights, stunts, or dangerous special effects—a substitute person takes the place of the principal actor. That person is known as a *double,* or a *stuntperson.* Usually doubles somewhat resemble the principals in physique; mainly they match the principals in height because height affects the lighting of a scene.

Scenes wherein doubles perform are always shot with a wide-angle lens, for the reason that the doubles are not recognizable from a distance. Thus the audience is unaware that it is not the stars who are performing the feats.

But in the coverage (close angles of the action), the principal actors step in, which gives the audience the impression that the stars are actually performing the risky business. Coverage is necessarily preplanned to take place at logical stages in the action (as rehearsed with the doubles). You should be extremely watchful at the fixed-action spots where the principal actors take over. Note, for instance, how the doubles land on the floor: the conspicuous position and the condition of the wardrobe and makeup. The principal actors also watch the doubles' performance so they can approximate their action. But your trained eye and careful notes are the acknowledged authority on the accuracy for coverage. Always indicate in your shot description and the Daily Editor's Log which shots were filmed with doubles.

COVERING MOVING SHOTS

When the camera physically moves—travels with actors as they walk and talk—an established rule is: Do not *cut into a moving camera* or a *moving actor.* For instance, the camera is following (moving with, or *trucking* with) two actors as they walk and talk. The director, in staging the scene, has decided beforehand which speeches and reactions will be made in single close shots, and instructs the actors to come to a halt at the beginning of each designated speech. The camera, too, must be stationary at the same moment. After the speeches have been delivered, both actors and camera resume moving in continuation of the scene. At a later time, the close shots will be covered at the exact spots where the stops were made.

You should make careful note of where the stops occurred: jot down a landmark, as well as some conspicuous background activity going on at the moment. A well-matched background enables the editor to effect smooth match-cuts into the master shot.

Technically, there is an alternative for cutting into a traveling shot: repeat the entire action with a closer lens on the moving camera. The editor will now have the option of intercutting the moving long shot with the moving close shot at judicious intervals.

A stationary camera in the process of a pan is the equivalent of a moving camera. You must always watch to see whether the camera head is in motion (panning or tilting) at a point where a cut-in of a close shot might be effective. Should the director desire to shoot a close shot at a point in the master shot where you happened to notice the camera was moving, you should quickly notify the director. The shot will be ruled out, and an alternative shot may be proposed. In any event, your alertness in preventing the unnecessary loss of time spent on a useless shot will be appreciated.

COVERING CLOSE-UPS

When filming close shots and close-ups, always be on the alert for off-camera actors' intrusions into a speech that will *overlap* (cut into) the dialogue of the actor on-camera. When that happens, a double voice is heard over the face of the actor being filmed, and the take has to be redone. Another thing to be aware of is off-camera laughter and crying within a scene. Such sounds tend to *trail* in the atmosphere (a sound phenomenon). Sometimes a trailing sound intrudes on the dialogue in the picture. It is advisable that you caution the off-camera actors to abruptly cut off their laughing and crying histrionics to ensure that the next on-camera speeches will be in the clear.

COVERING OFF-SCREEN OVERLAPS

During a performance, be alert for any off-screen noises that fall upon (overlap) a speech or action. Quickly mark your script where this has occurred. If the scene is not cut at that point, the director probably has made a mental note to cover that portion of the scene in another shot in order to eliminate the disturbance in the sound track. Sometimes, however, when concentrating on the performance, the director is oblivious to the overlapping noise. While it is advisable that you mention the overlap immediately after the take, you will undoubtedly hear the sound mixer yell, "There was an overlap!" and the director yell back, "It'll be covered." Thus, you know the director is aware of the situation. But make sure, before leaving the set, that there is indeed another shot to cover (eliminate) the off-screen (OS) disturbance. Always make notations in your continuity script as to which shots cover which overlaps. This will be very helpful to the editor.

COVERING WRONG ACTION

Following is a hypothetical series of shots. In one of the coverage shots a wrong action occurs that will disrupt the flow of smooth continuity editing (see Figure 10.5).

Frame No. 1: A wide-angle long shot is the master shot that encompasses all the action. The scene is that of a street with a woman in the background hurrying forward. She is carrying a suitcase in her right hand and a purse in her left hand. As she reaches the curb, she stops for a red light. When the light changes, she steps off the curb with her left foot and trips. This causes the woman to wince and the suitcase to fall to the ground. The woman recovers, picks up the suitcase, and continues across the street, running toward foreground camera and exiting the shot left-to-right (L–R). End of master shot.

Frame 2: A medium close shot. The woman stands at the curb waiting for the light to change. Thus she is introduced to the audience.

Frame 3: A tighter full shot at the curb. The woman steps off the curb, trips, and the suitcase falls. She winces with pain.

Frame 4: A big close-up. The woman's pained expression.

Frame 5: A low-angle shot. The woman bends down and picks up the suitcase.

Frame 6: A full shot. The woman steps off the curb and runs toward camera foreground left-to-right (L–R).

In repeating the action of the closer angles, it goes without saying that the woman's wardrobe and appearance must match in every detail. As to the performance, you must see to it that the woman steps off the curb with her left foot, that the suitcase falls approximately in the same position, and that she picks up the suitcase with the right hand and starts to run across the street toward camera left-to-right (L–R), at the same pace as in the master shot. (To repeat: when action in closer angles is matched as closely as possible to the master shot, it gives the illusion to the audience that the movements are continuous.)

Beware the Mismatch

Suppose that during the action in Frame 6 the woman unthinkingly switches the purse to her right hand and the suitcase to her left hand. All the camera directions are correct. However, there is an obvious action mismatch. If this shot were intercut with the last piece of the master shot, what would happen on the screen is this: in mid-run, the woman would suddenly and unaccountably be holding the suitcase in her left hand and the purse in her right hand (the reverse of Frame 8). This is known in the trade as a *movie boner*.

The Jump Cut

Sometimes a retake cannot be made on the spot—perhaps because gathering clouds changed the lighting of the area, or because the company was running into costly overtime.

Figure 10.5

Covering Wrong Action

Frame 1

Frame 2

Frame 3

Frame 4

Frame 5

Frame 6

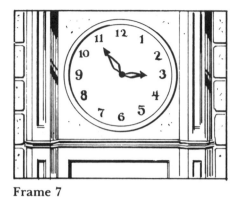

Frame 7   Frame 8

Without a retake to correct the mismatch, the editor will be forced to make a *jump cut*. That means the editor will have to cut out a piece of film from the master shot and the close full shot in order to make as smooth a transition as possible when joining (splicing) the two pieces of film. Conspicuous jump cuts cause jerky movements on the screen that are jarring to the audience.

> NOTE: The term *jump cut* differs in connotation from the term *jump on screen*. The latter refers to the jarring effect of incongruously juxtaposed props in a scene (see pages 158 and 159).

The Cutaway Shot

A conspicuous jump cut, or any kind of mismatch, can be remedied via the editorial strategy known as the *cutaway shot*—a quick cut from the flawed shot to a shot of an extraneous scene or object, or another person's reaction. Serving as a momentary distraction, the cutaway shot supports the possibility that a sudden, unaccountable change (such as a prop being in a character's left hand in one shot and right hand in the next shot) might reasonably have occurred during the interim occupied by the cutaway shot.

Consider the mismatch (boner) that occurred in the foregoing illustration. Let's assume that it was not possible, for whatever reason, to shoot a *retake* while the company was still in the setup. When met with this predicament, the editor's favorite tactic is the cutaway.

For example, at Frame 6 (showing the mismatch), the editor will cut the film at a judicious spot and insert a diversionary piece of film—perhaps a stock shot of a clock on a building (Frame 7), to give the audience the impression that time is of the essence in this scene. It can thus be assumed that during the brief period when the audience's attention is focused on the clock, the woman switches the purse to her left hand. To substantiate the switch, the editor will connect (splice) the shot of the clock with a judicious cut to the last piece of the master shot (Frame 8). It will not be apparent to the audience that the flow of continuity was interrupted. The mismatch in action will thus have been eliminated by cinematic illusion.

IMPORTANT: You must make a notation in your script to alert the editor of the wrong action, which resulted in the mismatch pictured in Frame 6. The editor will then resort to the stock-shot solution to make the scene viable.

One situation in which a technical snag cannot be rectified by a cutaway shot is when the shot is made with the camera in the wrong position—that is, when the camera has violated the 180° rule (see Chapter 9, under "Imaginary Line/Action Axis/180° Rule").

THE PROTECTION SHOT

From time to time, the director may decide to film a *protection shot*. This piece of film may or may not be used. The shot is made just in case there might be a problem that would otherwise mandate a costly retake.

- ☐ It may be advisable to film another angle of a shot as protection against some dubious footage, such as an action or direction mismatch.

- ☐ It is advisable to film a shot *both ways* when in doubt about a correct look (CR or CL); the editor will use the appropriate one.

- ☐ It is advisable to film some extraneous matter to use as a cutaway when some controversial footage, such as unseemly deportment or dialogue, will have to be excised.

- ☐ It is advisable to shoot extra coverage for a scene that was exceptionally complicated in staging, as protection against something untoward happening during the printing of the master shot.

When you have acquired a good sense of cinematic dramaturgy, you will be able to discern when a situation in a scene mandates a protection shot. And you will distinguish yourself by discreetly suggesting the filming of such critical shots to the director.

CUTTING IN THE CAMERA

A director may opt to film a lengthy scene in one master setup, without breaking up the shot—in effect, to pre-edit. This is achieved with a mobile camera, either mounted on a dolly or hand-held. The camera's ability to pan, tilt, and change focal lengths (zoom lens) is time-saving in that it dispenses with numerous coverage setups that would require resetting and relighting. But this manner of shooting mandates countless highly disciplined rehearsals on the part of the actors as well as the camera and sound technicians. All positions and every movement must be impeccably coordinated with flawless dialogue.

Cutting in the camera may do away with time-consuming coverage (and it spares the continuity supervisor the demanding task of matching the action in each setup). But it deprives the editor the luxury of choice and variation.

SHOOTING THE BEGINNING AND END OF A SCENE

Occasionally, to save time, the director will not shoot a master scene in its sequential entirety. Instead, a small segment at the start and end of the scene will be filmed with a wide-angle lens. These shots will establish the atmosphere and the spatial dimensions of the setting. Subsequently, the entire middle segment of the scene will be shot in tighter individual angles.

When this manner of shooting is practiced, it calls forth a filmic rule: Any scene or part of a scene that is put on film for the first time qualifies as a master shot. Consequently, you will have to carefully differentiate which portions of the middle section being filmed are indeed master shots and which are overlapped actions into the previously filmed beginning and end of the scene. Shooting in this fragmented style exercises your skills in matching action and, particularly, in calculating picture-running time.

COVERING ALTERNATIVE MASTER SHOTS

If you have complied with the instructions under "Alternative Shots" in Chapter 5, you will have made notes on how each of the printed master shots differed in business, dialogue, and camera perspectives and made the respective action-matching notes for both performances. So you are prepared to do battle with coverage.

But first you must ascertain which of the two masters the director wishes to cover. If time and budget permit, it is indeed preferable to obtain coverage on both master shots. In that way, the editor has the luxury of utilizing the best segments of each master with its respective cover shots. It goes without saying that if both master shots are to be covered (director's prerogative), there is double demand on your matching skills.

INTERCUTTING TELEPHONE CONVERSATIONS

As described in Chapter 5 under "Timing the Performance," each character in a telephone conversation is shot individually. A filmic convention is to film the characters as though they are facing each other: one looks camera-right and the other looks camera-left. While this rule is sometimes violated (with impunity), we shall consider it a basic principle.

Make it a habit to note the camera direction (look) of the character who is filmed first (but who may not be the first to speak, scriptwise). Alongside that name, note "Look CL" (or CR, as the case may be); then immediately make notation of the opposite look beside the other character's name (see Figure 10.6). In this way, during the filming of the second character (usually at a later date), you will know instantly what the correct look should be for that character. This will save you the trouble of frantically thumbing through your script notes to find the clue.

Figure 10.6

JANET *(Look CR)*
Hello, may I speak to Mr. Smith?

MR. SMITH *(Look CL)*
This is Mr. Smith.

11

Techniques of Matching

ACTION MATCHING/THE MATCH CUT

As mentioned in Chapter 10, the cinematic principles of coverage and action matching are inextricably linked. The concept of action matching originated when early cinematographers (now titled directors of photography) and film editors (then titled cutters) sought a filmic formula to effect a transition of movement that would make the shift from one shot to another as imperceptible to the audience as possible and obviate the *jump cut*.

The discipline that evolved led to the axiom "Cut on action" (or "Cut on movement"). In other words, plan to cut from the master shot to another angle when subjects are in motion—rising from a sitting or kneeling position, sitting or falling from a standing position, making conspicuous hand gestures or body turns (see "What the Continuity Supervisor Oversees" in Chapter 1; see also "Overt Action" under "How to Break Down a Script" in Chapter 2).

> NOTE: The term *cut on action* (or *cut on movement*) is not to be confused with the terms *cut into a moving actor* or *cut into a moving camera,* as discussed in Chapter 10 under "Covering Moving Shots." From the standpoint of cinematic technology, the two circumstances are unrelated.

To ensure editing continuity, the matching of action mandates that the movement and dialogue from portions of the master shot be meticulously duplicated. The most harmonious transition into the master shot from a

183

close shot is achieved when the repeated action in the close shot starts from a few feet ahead of the spot where the cut in the master shot is planned and continues for a few feet beyond the cut in the master shot. The small amount of overlapping footage at the beginning and end of the closer shot provides the editor with essential footage to effect a more precise cut (action match) when joining (splicing) the close shot with the master shot. The result is the illusion of uninterrupted movement in a continuous flow of film.

The technique of overlapping action applies also when making pick-up shots in a flawed master shot (see "The Bridge Shot" in Chapter 5).

The task of action matching has become one of the preeminent functions of the continuity supervisor. During the staging and rehearsals of the master shot, you can usually discern where cut-ins with closer angles would serve as interesting dramatic punctuation. You (and the director) should know from which points the overlapping footage of action and dialogue should start and end.

With experience, you will acquire a keen sense of cinematic dramaturgy and be able to recognize readily which actions and dialogue have potential for closer angles. The editor's artful splicing of all the pieces of film into smooth-flowing continuity is the culmination of artfully matched action and dialogue during the performance.

ACTORS AND MATCHING *

Some years ago, the popular actress Ellen Corby ("The Waltons") gave me a gift of a short poem that she wrote when she was a "script girl" in the "good old days." I've recited it on numerous occasions in my career.

> When I ask you to match your action
> Why do you refuse it?
> What's the good of a close-up
> If the cutter can't use it?

It helps immeasurably if actors are cognizant of their movements during master scenes and repeat their actions exactly as many times as required for every angle being shot. But because actors are historically not faithful to this discipline, it is up to you to carefully communicate to them what they did in previous shots. Highly professional film actors usually match all details as closely to the original as possible. But less seasoned actors require a little more coaching.

---

* A word of caution: some actors don't like to be reminded of their movements and some directors don't like you to talk at length to the actors. So you communication skills are on the line!

Occasionally, a problem arises when actors do not consistently match their movements and dialogue from shot to shot. After several unsuccessful takes, an actor may object to repeating again and again an ill-matched take. You will hear the expression, "Oh, use one or the other." This is partly valid because the image can appear on the screen only once, but it is not always the best solution. A mismatch or a transposition of words forces the editor to make a crucial choice. The take in which the actor achieved a perfect action match may not contain the best reading of the speech or the best dramatic interpretation of the scene. In opting to use the best dialogue take, the editor may face the dilemma of a jarring *jump cut* in the action. On the other hand, if the editor opts for the better action match and leaves the actor's more compelling delivery on the cutting-room floor, the audience will never know that the actor is capable of a stronger performance. If film actors learned and practiced the art of matching, they could ensure their best performance on screen at all times. And it would make the continuity supervisor's task a little easier.

It is humanly impossible and patently unnecessary to simultaneously watch and note every detail in a scene. The mark of a competent continuity supervisor is not the possession of extraordinary powers of observation (although that is valuable) but knowing what is important to observe for matching purposes. By the same token, knowing when it is *not* necessary to match certain details proves invaluable. It saves the actors' vexation and the company's time (which translates into money).

MATCHING BACKGROUND

The matching of background action is not in your sphere of responsibility; it belongs to the first and second assistant directors. Nevertheless, it is good policy, and to your advantage, to keep an eye on the background, particularly if the business there is conspicuous.

Background (BG) and foreground (FG) action usually involves extras. The most important factor in matching background is to know on which speeches in the master shot the extras crossed behind or in front of the principal actors, and whether they were moving camera left-to-right or right-to-left. Your concern for matching background details in every angle will be appreciated by the editor.

PRECISION MATCHING
FOR CLOSE-UPS

It is a foregone conclusion that wardrobe, makeup, and hair must match flawlessly in every angle. But there are additional elements in close-ups that require strict fidelity to the master shot (see "Overt Action" under "How to Break Down a Script" in Chapter 2). Watch for:

☐ The actor bending backward, forward, or sideways.

☐ A puff of a cigarette made at the same point in dialogue, with the cigarette held in the same hand and smoked to the same size.

☐ A pipe placed in the same corner of the mouth every time it is put in or taken out of the mouth.

☐ The contents and color of liquid in a glass, with the glass held in the same hand and the sip taken at the same point in the dialogue.

☐ An object or another person's hand brought up to the cheek or shoulder of the subject in close-up and taken away at the exact same time in a manner corresponding to the original direction (camera right-to-left or left-to-right).

☐ Shoulders or torsos crossing behind or in front of the subject, timed exactly to the action in the master.

UNNECESSARY MATCHING

As mentioned earlier, a competent continuity supervisor knows when not to waste time and energy on nonessentials. In a close-shot setup, if a person or an object was seen in the master wide-angle shot positioned at the side, below, or above the close-up subject, those peripheral components may be out of frame. It is unnecessary to match any of those details because they are not seen in the close-up frame. The criterion is *knowing exactly what the frame is holding*.

As mentioned in Chapter 9 under "Inscribed Area," it is your prerogative, at all times, to peer into the camera and see the image in the frame. And don't always depend on the camera operator's response when you ask what the frame is holding. When you see the dailies—or, worse, the finished film—you may discover, to your dismay, that the frame encompassed a slightly larger area than the operator had indicated. And you will agonize (vainly) over the fact that a portion of a body or a prop belonged in that space.

MATCHING RUNNING SHOTS

When the action of a scene involves actors running progressively from one shot (locale) to another, it is essential that the actors match the pace and breathing sounds of each preceding running shot, no matter how much time elapses between setups. The first shot of a running sequence may be filmed in the early morning and the subsequent ones filmed hours, or even days and weeks, later. It is not unusual for an actor to begin a shot by running from distance, skipping rope, or hopping in place until he or she attains the same degrees of speed and breathlessness captured in the preceding shot.

MATCH DISSOLVES

When the image at the end of a shot is designed to parallel that at the beginning of another shot filmed at a different locale or time, it is known as a *match dissolve*. Following are a few hypothetical examples:

☐ The scene is of a street accident. We see an injured person placed on an ambulance gurney. The camera Zooms In, or Dissolves, to a close-up of the injured face (with makeup simulating blood and wounds). The next shot (probably filmed weeks later) opens on a matching close-up of the injured face. Now the camera Zooms Out, or Pulls Back, to a Medium or Full shot and reveals the gurney in another Exterior location—now at the emergency entrance to a hospital, and then wheeled to the inside. The image at the start of the second shot must be the same size and have the same makeup as the face in the Match Dissolve filmed at the scene of the accident.

   If the hospital-locale scene is shot first (as is likely to be the case), the makeup and simulated accident details, as well as the size of the shot, will have to be matched when filming the scene of the accident on the street.

☐ The scene is of a couple kissing on a cruise ship. The camera Dissolves to a two-head Close-up (kissing). The next shot is a similar two-head Close-up. But as the camera Zooms Out, or Pulls Back, the scene is a suburban living room, and the man is kissing a different woman—his wife.

☐ The scene is of a man dropping a pellet into a glass of water placed on a nightstand. The camera Dissolves to an insert of the pellet disintegrating in the water. The next shot opens on an insert of the glass, and as the camera Zooms Out, or Pulls Back, to a medium shot, we see a woman lift the glass and drink from it. The implication is that the woman is being poisoned.

When the script indicates, or the director designs, Match Dissolves, it is essential that you keep a record of the lens sizes and the distances between the subjects and the camera. This will expedite the setting up of the subsequent matching shots.

   An example of a superb match dissolve and parallel action sequence was displayed in the television miniseries "The Thorn Birds." (*Parallel action* means alternating two contrasting episodes that take place concurrently in a story. It adds poignancy and excitement to the sequence.)

In "The Thorn Birds," the priest, Ralph, who denies his love for Meggie, is taking his vows as bishop while Meggie is taking her marriage vows to Luke, a man she does not love. The successive shots of the two presiding priests uttering almost identical vows in two diametrically opposed circumstances were fraught with tension. Ralph saying "I will" was followed by a quick cut to Meggie whispering "I will." The height of poignancy came when the camera focused on a big close-up of the bishop's ring being slipped onto Ralph's finger and then dissolved to a matching shot of a wedding ring being slipped onto Meggie's finger. It was a splendid example of editing.

As stated earlier, masterful action-match cutting can be achieved if the editor is given film that has been masterfully action-matched in the performance.

WHAT AND HOW TO OBSERVE FOR MATCHING

The following is a lengthy but only partial list of the numerous minute details that demand your acute observation. NOTE: I use an easy format for directional notations in my continuity script. To indicate parts of the body, I write L-side, R-side, L-hand, R-hand, etc. To indicate positions for the camera, I write CL and CR (the right side of the body is CL for camera, and the left side of the body is CR for camera). It is best to tell an actor that his hair was parted on the right side of his head, or tell an actress that the belt was tied to her left side. This will make it automatically correct for the camera.

Watch Hands

. . . into pants pockets: R or L or both; when placed into and when taken out of pockets; note whether jacket corners are in front or behind pants pockets.

. . . buttoning and unbuttoning jackets, coats, shirts.

. . . holding props: cigarettes, cigars, pipes, drinking glasses, eyeglasses (when put on and when taken off during dialogue).

. . . wearing jewelry: rings on fingers, bracelets, watches, cuff links.

. . . picking up articles: cup, with or without saucer (on what word); and sip taken before or after which word in dialogue.

. . . placed on hips: put up on which word, taken down on which word.

. . . placed on doors being opened and closed.

. . . holding telephones: R-hand to R-ear; L-hand to L-ear; R-hand to L-ear; L-hand to R-ear; hand over mouthpiece.

. . . gloves: wearing both; wearing one, on which hand, and which hand holds the other; taking gloves off, which hand first.

. . . arms folded: L over R or R over L; tucked under armpits, or holding elbows.

. . . pale skin in close-ups (should have body makeup).

. . . holding letters and envelopes or other objects.

. . . handing objects to another actor or receiving objects from off camera: with which hand; position of object.

. . . placed on objects when making insert shots.

. . . picking up objects: with R or L hand, from CR or CL.

. . . arms around another person: at waist, on shoulder; placed at which point during dialogue or action; when removed.

. . . sleeves; rolled up or pushed up; cuffs buttoned or open.

. . . holding pencils and pens (in which hand; pointing in which direction).

. . . nail polish: color and condition.

Watch Babes in Arms

. . . held in R or L arm; or R or L shoulder; how swaddling clothes are arranged; how blankets are wrapped.

Watch Hair

. . . hair style: parted on R-side or L-side; slant of bangs.

. . . women's long hair: on which shoulder strands of hair fall to front.

. . . pushed behind which ear.

. . . little girls' braids and curls: falling which way as they turn and twist.

Watch Bodies in Bed

. . . which way head lies: R-profile or L-profile, or facing upward.

. . . position of pillows: open end of pillowcase to CR or CL (toward center of bed or at sides).

. . . position of covers: amount of sheet lapped over blanket; covers pulled up to which part of body.

. . . woman's hair spread on pillow.

Watch Rising and Sitting Positions

. . . on which word person sat down or stood up; note dialogue in standing and sitting positions; watch level of eyes directed toward off-camera dialogue for each position.

Watch Legs

. . . crossed at knees, R over L or L over R; does knee extend horizontally?

. . . crossed at ankles, R over L or L over R.

Watch Turns

. . . head moves to R or L shoulder (CR or CL).

. . . body turns on R or L shoulder.

> NOTE: In shooting over-the-shoulder shots, turns of the head and body are crucial. Editing cuts are usually made on turns.

Watch Body Leaning

. . . forward or backward, or to the sides CL or CR.

Watch Fight Scenes and Stunts

. . . actions of doubles to be repeated by principals.

. . . arrangement of clothing.

. . . end positions of falls.

Watch Stubble on Men's Faces

. . . days of growth according to script chronology.

Watch Injuries

. . . progressive makeup and bandaging according to script chronology.

Watch Walking

. . . for matching overt gestures made while in movement.

Watch Stairs

. . . actors' pace walking or running up or down; if stop is made, note on which step and what action, if any.

. . . which way actors make turns at top or bottom landings, exiting shot CR or CL.

Watch Falling Objects

. . . dropping down CL or CR.

Watch Picking Up Objects

. . . with R- or L-hand, from CR or CL.

Watch Eating Scenes

. . . handling of dishes and utensils; note kind of food.

Watch Entrances and Exits

. . . lineup of people; pace.

. . . carrying of props.

Watch Wardrobe

. . . men's ties: position of knot (beware diagonal stripes).

. . . men's shirts: collar button open or closed; button-downs open or buttoned.

. . . ring around the collar (makeup soil): garment must be changed if noticeable in camera.

. . . men's pajamas under robes: collar in or out; L-hand or R-hand corner protruding.

. . . men's pocket handkerchief: match arrangement.

. . . men's hats: position on head; brim up or down; cocked to L or R side; held in which hand and in what position; crown or hollow to camera.

. . . collar positions: turned up or down.

. . . scarves or neckerchiefs: tied to L-side or R-side.

Watch Accessories

. . . earrings, necklaces.

. . . shoulder ornaments.

. . . belts: buckled to R or L side; tied in a bow or knot, to L or R side.

. . . ladies' handbags: held in which hand, or over which shoulder; note switching from hand to hand.

Watch Props

. . . time on clock: if story point, see that hands move; reset for every passage of time.

. . . dates on calendars: according to the script or mentioned in dialogue.

. . . liquid in glasses: note level of fullness; match color.

. . . books: inquire whether identification needs to be hidden (clearance may be required); if open to recognizable page in master, match for close-up.

. . . lamps: lit or unlit.

. . . candles: lit or unlit; positions and sizes.

Watch Doors

. . . placement in set: at BG or CR or CL side walls.

. . . which way they open: toward or away from camera (indicate with arrows).

. . . double doors: which side opens and closes (indicate with arrows).

. . . when shoooting at doors from EXT to INT and vice versa, see that the door hinges are hung properly: a diagram of the position of the door-knob will ensure correct opening and closing when shooting between INT and EXT.

. . . position of door: open, closed, or ajar—before, during, or after action.

. . . glass doors: legends and numbers to correspond with script; record what is seen on other side.

Watch Windows

. . . placement in set: on which wall (BG, CL, or CR).

. . . draperies and blinds: fully or partially drawn, open or closed.

. . . shades: halfway up, down, or which way.

Watch Furniture

. . . placement in relation to camera angles.

. . . position of chairs: seats or backs to camera.

. . . props placed on furniture: over backs or arms, or across seats of chairs and sofas. Match the way garments have been folded.

. . . pillows on sofas and chairs: placement and color rotation.

Watch Set Dressing

. . . in close-up angles, note details in BG or FG, or at the sides of the person or object being photographed.

Watch Automobiles

. . . match close shots to traveling long shots.

. . . elbows or hands on door windows.

. . . hand positions on steering wheel.

Watch Legends on Buildings

. . . numbers and logos: to correspond with dialogue or business mentioned in script.

12

Second-Unit
Filming

At times, your assignment may be with the second unit of a company. The second unit shoots designated script scenes that have been separated from the first unit's schedule: scenes of large crowds that may or may not include principal actors, outdoor activities, chases, horse or automobile ride-bys, special stunts with doubles, or extraneous panoramic scenery. Sometimes the second unit comprises a full crew, but usually it's a skeleton crew with its own second-unit director and continuity supervisor.

Your involvement with preparation and script breakdown is of course minimal compared to that of the first-unit continuity supervisor. Although your responsibilities are within the bounds of the second-unit sequences, it is advisable that you study the One Line prepared by the first-unit supervisor. This will familiarize you with the whole story.

There may be scenes wherein the second-unit operation includes shots that will intercut with the principal filming. Let's assume that a principal actor rides out of a close shot on a horse at a walk or a trot. He is wearing a brown jacket and a tan hat, and he is mounted on a sorrel horse that is covered with a maroon blanket. The double in the second unit continues the shot (in a wide angle) and accelerates to a faster pace. Of course, the double cannot be seen wearing a checkered jacket and a brown hat and riding a pinto horse covered with a plaid blanket. Clothing and props are furnished for the doubles. Your responsibility, unequivocally, is to make sure that the double starts at the same pace and follows in the same screen direction as the principal: camera right-to-left or left-to-right.

Even more critical is when the second unit is scheduled to shoot an intergrated sequence before the first unit does so. In that case, both continuity supervisors must meticulously coordinate their notes to cover every detail. As second continuity supervisor, you will obtain wardrobe and props records from those departments. But I caution you to compare these with the records of the first continuity supervisor: there's many a slip between the horse and the whip.

SECOND-UNIT SLATING

The system of slate numbering, of course, must conform to that of the first unit. In other words, either scene-number or consecutive-number slating must be used by both units. With scene-number slating, there is no problem: the second unit uses the designated scene numbers. However, with consecutive-numbered slating, the second-unit operation starts with a very high number (e.g., 5,000) to ensure that there is no conflict with the first unit's numbers. The numbers on the slate tell the editor which shots are from the first or the second unit.

As second-unit continuity supervisor, you will keep separate records of scene count, page count, and picture time. You will turn your records over to the first-unit supervisor, together with all your pertinent continuity notes. The first-unit supervisor will combine the notes of both units and make a comprehensive record of all the film footage and sound tracks for the editor.

13

Television Series

EPISODIC SHOWS

Compared with feature films, television shows demand more intensive work on the part of all members of the crew and cast. Shows have to be completed in time for air dates, so the pace of shooting and editing is greatly accelerated. Yet the necessary time for careful preparation is limited. The result is long workdays under heavy pressure.

SHOOTING BACK TO BACK

Weekly television shows are usually shot *back to back*. That means the shows are shot continuously, without any time between the end of one show and the start of another. This operation necessitates that you break down the second script while still in the process of shooting the first. Back to back shooting makes for longer workdays and fattened paychecks (you get additional prep-time pay), but you are deprived of time for careful preparation.*

---

* Some companies alternate continuity supervisors when shooting episodic shows. Naturally, one does not earn as much pay under such an arrangement. Nevertheless, there are those continuity supervisors who welcome the relief from constant pressures—and the time to indulge in more pleasurable pursuits.

To ensure your utmost control in shooting two shows back to back, it is advisable to prepare each script according to all the breakdown rules described for a single script. You may cheat a little, but only to resourcefully cut some corners in the interest of time. The important thing is to be so prepared that you can function on both shows with complete confidence and equanimity—even if bothered by a touch of anxiety.

SHOOTING MULTIPLE SHOWS

Shooting two shows back to back is a snap compared with working multiple shows. The latter means shooting bits and pieces from two, three, or as many as ten or twelve scripts in one day. The "My Three Sons" series was produced in this manner. For eight years I was the continuity supervisor. The operation was as follows:

The star of the show worked the first eight weeks of a thirty-six-week schedule. In that period of time, we shot, on a daily basis, scenes and portions of scenes from twelve to fifteen scripts. In each master setup, whenever feasible, a second camera simultaneously photographed the star's close-ups. If other portions of scenes that included the star needed coverage, those shots were also made during this initial period. One or two days a week, we filmed the outdoor sequences in which the star appeared. For instance: the star comes out of the front door of the house, crosses to the carport, gets into the car, and drives away. In the same setup, the star drives the automobile from the street to the carport, crosses to the front door, and goes inside. We shot these two actions (dad going to work; dad coming home from work) until we had completed the number of times this action was described in each of the scripts. For each separate sequence, the star had a change of wardrobe so it would be compatible with the interior scenes of each script.

Example of shooting in another locale—the kitchen: we filmed, consecutively, six to eight breakfast scenes, eight to ten luncheon scenes (the kids always came home for lunch), and as many dinner scenes as were written into the scripts. The property master had to match all the different foods that were displayed (and eaten) in the master scenes; I had to match the various morsels of food on the dishes that were served to the children at each meal. The makeup department had to match all the boys' haircuts and injuries that happened in the master scenes. The wardrobe department had the problem of matching garments that the boys outgrew between the master scenes with the star and the portions of scenes shot later. To match parts of scenes that were filmed months earlier, the pants, shirts, and jackets had to be altered or duplicated.

This manner of shooting was a colossal undertaking for the production manager and the first assistant director. After perspicaciously preparing the production boards, the weekly Shooting Schedules, and the Daily Call

Sheets, they faced the constant need to alter the routines in order to meet the daily, inevitable variables in the scheduling of sets and in the actors' and children's availability. Also picture the film editor's predicament of holding, in suspended animation—for months—strips of film for more than a dozen unfinished shows and working on them sporadically as added shots were supplied, until one of the scripts was finally completed. Nor were the directors' efforts anything less than prodigious.

The tasks of scene matching and action matching for multiple scenes out of multiple scripts, shot three and four months apart, was a stupendous exercise—not to mention the clerical logistics of providing daily progress reports on perhaps a dozen scripts: reconciling page and scene counts, number of setups, and picture time on scripts shot intermittently over a period of months. The gimmicks that the department heads devised for keeping viable continuity notes became an art form.

At the end of forty days or so, we were into thirty shows, having shot all the exterior and interior scenes in which the star appeared. During the next several months, we continued filming at the rate of ten to twelve scripts a day. We shot all the other scenes in the unfinished scripts, and shot coverage for all the scenes that corresponded with the star's earlier close-up shots. At this juncture, both the dialogue coach (we had one, of course, to coach all those kids) and I read the star's off-camera dialogue to the actors being filmed. In this fashion, we completed all the remaining scenes in all the partially filmed scripts.

Many years ago, Western serials were shot in this manner, but hardly with that many scripts in one day, and surely not with the star absent for the greater part of the shooting schedule; nor was there any urgency then to meet air time.

Appendix C does not include the complex forms that were devised for this unique operation, because it is not likely that another production company will imitate the procedure. If one does, and you get the assignment, it will be excellent experience for you to devise the necessary forms.

14

Epilogue

YOUR CAREER WARDROBE*

When continuity supervising is your career, you will need to keep suitable outfits readily accessible in your closets for every weather condition in every season of the year. Depending upon your location assignment, you may, in a single day, run the gamut from heavy winter garments down to a pair of shorts or a swim suit. Experience will teach you a practical design for dressing: put your clothes on in layers.

Let me tell you about one assignment. The location was the San Bernardino Mountains in California. It is known that the temperature there goes from 32°F in the morning to about 104° at midday, and drops to about 40° at night. My attire in the morning consisted of thermal underwear, a medium-weight skirt (or pants), and a cotton T-shirt; over that a short-sleeved blouse; over that a long-sleeved blouse; over that a sweater; and all of this topped with a windbreaker or fur jacket and a scarf. In my tote bag were several hats.

As the freezing morning thawed, I started my striptease act. At midday, when the heat was at its height, I was down to T-shirt, shorts, and straw hat. Then as the sun set and we worked through the freezing hours of the night, I started to put the garments back on again.

---

* If you purchase special clothing for your work, check with your income tax counselor; the expense may be tax deductible.

It's a good idea to keep a supply of hats: woolen ones to keep your head and ears warm against freezing temperatures or howling winds; cotton ones for mild days; and brimmed straw ones to keep your nose from being scorched and your hair from turning flaxen from the sun. Other useful items to keep available are light and heavy rain and snow gear. *Semper paratus.*

A PERSONAL WORD

The continuity supervisor is a highly visible person on the set. Your deportment and appearance should at all times reflect decorum and neatness. This is true for the men as well as the women. Performing your job with competence and dignity will merit you an enviable reputation.

SCREEN CREDIT

Through an inexplicable miscarriage of contract negotiations over the years, the International Alliance of Theatrical and Stage Employees (IATSE), in dealing with the Producers' Association panel, has been unsuccessful in negotiating screen credit for the important craft of script supervising—a recognition that entails no monetary costs for the producer.

Back in April 1965, *Daily Variety* printed a letter I had addressed to the editor in response to a tribute paid to the craftspeople behind the camera. The craft of the script supervisor had been omitted. My letter stated: "Script supervisors make invaluable contributions in the preparation and shooting of a motion picture . . . they are the most unsung heroes and heroines on the set . . . and it is regrettable that script supervisors do not receive screen credit by union contract."

In recent years, script (continuity) supervisors have been awarded screen credit. But there are production managers who still cling to the letter of the antiquated contract and deny screen credit.

The glaring inequity prevails because, for the most part, producers and others in executive positions are not cognizant of the intrinsic part the continuity supervisor plays in the making of a film. Why? Because a skilled continuity supervisor unobtrusively makes significant corrections and improvements in the script and in the performance before the camera starts to roll, thus preventing incongruities from appearing on the screen.

And there are other areas in which the multiskilled continuity supervisor saves inestimable company costs:

☐ In the figuring of picture time. When inaccurate timing results in a show that is too short, the expense of writing and shooting additional scenes is incurred. When inaccurate timing results in a show that is too long, the editor has to devote many overtime hours (at immense company expense) to trim sequences and bring the film to acceptable length. Cutting out scenes, or parts of scenes, from a film causes jumps on the screen that disturb the flow of continuity and distract the audience's attention from the action and dialogue.

☐ In knowing when to reload the camera. The camera assistant may ask whether 175 feet in the magazine will make the next shot. At this point in time, several things have to be considered. If 175 feet will make the shot, there's the question of whether the take should be made before the lunch break, which would risk going into *meal penalty* (overtime pay to actors and crew). The first assistant director consults the continuity supervisor and, within seconds, the decision is made to delay the take until after the lunch period, thus saving the company a substantial amount of penalty monies.

If the shot cannot be made with the small amout of film in the magazine, the company may realize some money by selling the raw stock. Accumulations of short ends are sold to small independent filmmakers, to colleges for student projects, etc.

☐ In cuing actors. By skilfully rehearsing and cuing actors, the continuity supervisor saves the company inestimable costs. Thorough rehearsals preclude the repetition of flawed takes. This in turn curtails expenses on production time, film footage, and sound tape.

☐ When shooting is done away from the studio. At such times, the continuity supervisor assumes a responsibility that goes unrecognized by the production office. When filming takes place in a room of a private home or a place of business, the work area is confined to four walls instead of the studio's convenient three-walled set. The room gets crammed with camera equipment, and little space is left for personnel. Only the actors, director, director of photography, camera operator and assistant, sound mixer, and continuity supervisor squeeze into the room. Often, even the first assistant director is not included. During the performance, extemporaneous actions may displace a prop, change a hairdo, take off or put on a piece of clothing, alter a scar or bruise in makeup, etc. Any of the above may affect other scenes. Consequently, it is encumbent upon the continuity supervisor to convey to each of the department heads what notations need to be made in their respective records to ensure continuity matching for any contingent scenes.

It is this author's hope that, henceforth, the continuity supervisor's contribution to the filmmaking process will be acknowledged with screen credit guaranteed by contract—and that the screen credit will display the most appropriate title: Continuity Supervisor.

Appendix A

Abbreviations for Shot Descriptions

ANG:	Angle
ARRI:	Arriflex
BG (Bg):	Background
BH/CU:	Big head close-up
CH/SH:	Choker shot
CL:	Camera left
COMP:	Complete
CONT:	Continued
CR:	Camera right
CS:	Close shot
CU:	Close-up
D/A:	Down angle
D/B:	Dolly back
D/I:	Dolly in
DIAL:	Dialogue
DISS:	Dissolve
DBLE:	Double
ECU:	Extreme close-up
ELS:	Extreme long shot
ENT:	Enter
E/S:	End slate
EST:	Establish shot
EXT:	Exterior

FG (Fg):	Foreground
F/I:	Fade in
F/O:	Fade out
FS:	False start
F/SH:	Full shot
FT:	Feet
F2/SH:	Full two shot
F3/SH:	Full three shot
GR/SH:	Group shot
H/A:	High angle
INC:	Incomplete
INT:	Interior
L/A:	Low angle
L/SH:	Long shot
L–R:	Left-to-right
MAST:	Master shot
MCU:	Medium close-up
MCS:	Medium close shot
MED:	Medium shot
MLS:	Medium long shot
MOS:	Film without sound track
MS:	Medium shot
NG:	No good
OC:	Off-Camera
OS:	Off-Screen
OV/SH:	Over the Shoulder
P/B:	Pull back
PL/B:	Playback
P/I:	Push In
R–L:	Right-to-left
R/SH:	Rake shot
SC:	Scene
SGLE/FS:	Single full shot
SND:	Sound
SFX:	Sound effects
SPFX:	Special effects
T/SH (TITE SH):	Tight shot
TR/SH:	Tracking (or trucking) shot
TRAV/SH:	Traveling shot
W/A:	Wide angle
X/ANG:	Cross angle
X'S:	Crosses screen
X'T:	Exits shot
Z/I:	Zoom in
Z/O:	Zoom out

Appendix B

Conversions

Conversion Table

35mm film runs through the camera at:
90 Feet per Minute (fpm) (60 seconds)
24 Frames per Second (fps)
16 Frames per Foot (fpf)

Converting Footage to Time:

(Film ran 298 ft.)

Divide number of feet by 90

$$\begin{array}{r} 3 \\ 90\overline{)298} \\ \underline{270} = 3 \text{ min.} \\ +28 \text{ ft*} \end{array}$$

*To determine seconds on less than 90 feet:

Deduct 1/3 from number of feet; the answer equals the number of seconds:

$$\begin{array}{r} 28 \text{ ft.} \\ -\ 9\ 1/3 \\ \hline 18\ 2/3 \text{ seconds} \end{array}$$

Thus:

298 ft. = 3 min. & 18 2/3 sec.

Also written as: 3′ 18 2/3″

Converting Time to Footage:

(Film ran 3 min. & 18 2/3 sec.)

Multiply minutes by 90

$$\begin{array}{r} 3 \text{ min.} \quad = 270 \text{ ft.} \\ 18\ 2/3 \text{ sec.} = \underline{28 \text{ ft.*}} \\ 298 \text{ ft.} \end{array}$$

*To determine footage on less than 1 minute (60 seconds):

Add 1/2 to the number of seconds; the answer equals the number of feet:

$$\begin{array}{r} 18\ 2/3 \text{ sec.} \\ +\ 9\ 1/3 \\ \hline 28 \text{ feet} \end{array}$$

Thus:

3 min. & 18 2/3 sec. = 298 ft.

The fractions may be rounded out for quick calculation
(1 foot is less than 1 second: 1½ ft. per sec.)

$$\begin{array}{r} 28 \text{ ft.} \\ -\ 9 \\ \hline 19 \text{ seconds} \end{array} \qquad \begin{array}{r} 19 \text{ sec.} \\ +\ 9 \\ \hline 28 \text{ feet} \end{array}$$

Conversion Chart

Seconds	35mm Footage	Minutes	35mm Footage
1	1½	1	90
2	3	2	180
3	4½	3	270
4	6	4	360
5	7½	5	450
6	9	6	540
7	10½	7	630
8	12	8	720
9	13½	9	810
10	15	10	900
11	16½	11	990
12	18	12	1080
13	19½	13	1170
14	21	14	1260
15	22½	15	1350
16	24	16	1440
17	25½	17	1530
18	27	18	1620
19	28½	19	1710
20	30	20	1800
21	31½	21	1890
22	33	22	1980
23	34½	23	2070
24	36	24	2160
25	37½	25	2250
26	39	26	2340
27	40½	27	2430
28	42	28	2520
29	43½	29	2610
30	45	30	2700
31	46½	31	2790
32	48	32	2880
33	49½	33	2970
34	51	34	3060
35	52½	35	3150
36	54	36	3240
37	55½	37	3330
38	57	38	3420
39	58½	39	3510
40	60	40	3600
41	61½	41	3690
42	63	42	3780
43	64½	43	3870
44	66	44	3960
45	67½	45	4050
46	69	46	4140
47	70½	47	4230
48	72	48	4320
49	73½	49	4410
50	75	50	4500
51	76½	51	4590
52	78	52	4680
53	79½	53	4770
54	81	54	4860
55	82½	55	4950
56	84	56	5040
57	85½	57	5130
58	87	58	5220
59	88½	59	5310
60 (1 Min.)	90	60 (1 Hr.)	5400

Appendix C

Sample Forms

DAILY CONTINUITY LOG

PRODUCTION NO._____   DATE_____
TITLE_____   WORK DAY_____

FORWARD

Shoot. Call_____

	CAM ROL	SND ROL	SET UP	SCENE	SLATE	PRNT	TIME	TOTL TIME	PAGES	TOTL PAGES
1st Shot_____										
Lunch_____										
1st Shot_____										
Dinner_____										
1st Shot_____										
Cam. Wrap_____										
Snd Wrap_____										
Scenes Covered										
Wild Tracks										
Retakes										

	Scenes	Pages
Total Script_____		
Added_____		
Deleted_____		
New Total_____		
Shot Prior_____		
Shot Today_____		
To Date_____		
To Do_____		

TOTAL
FORWARD

DAILY EDITOR'S LOG

DATE_____   TITLE_____
WORK DAY_____   DIRECTOR_____
PROD. NO._____

CAM ROL	SND ROL	SET	SCENE#	SLATE#	PRINT	TIME	DESCRIPTION

WILD TRACKS   REMARKS

Continuity Supervisor

DAILY PROGRESS REPORT

Shoot. Call_____   Date_____

1st Shot_____   Work Day_____

Lunch_____   Prod. No._____

1st Shot_____   Title_____

Dinner_____   Director_____

1st Shot_____

Cam. Wrap_____

Snd Wrap_____

	Scenes	Pages	Minutes	Setups
Total Script	_____	_____	_____	_____
Added	_____	_____	_____	_____
Deleted	_____	_____	_____	_____
New Total	_____	_____	_____	_____
Shot Prior	_____	_____	_____	_____
Shot Today	_____	_____	_____	_____
To Date	_____	_____	_____	_____
To do	_____	_____		

Scenes Covered	Wild Tracks	Retakes	Remarks

Continuity Supervisor

212

STORY CHRONOLOGY/TIME BREAKDOWN

TITLE:_____

SCENE NOS.	TIME
_____	_____
_____	_____
_____	_____
_____	_____
_____	_____
_____	_____
_____	_____
_____	_____
_____	_____
_____	_____
_____	_____
_____	_____
_____	_____
_____	_____
_____	_____
_____	_____
_____	_____
_____	_____
_____	_____

SCENE COUNT

TITLE:_____

_____
_____
_____
_____
_____
_____
_____
_____
_____
_____
_____
_____
_____
_____
_____
_____
_____
_____
_____
_____
_____
_____
_____

214

PAGE COUNT

TITLE:_____

_____
_____
_____
_____
_____
_____
_____
_____
_____
_____
_____
_____
_____
_____
_____
_____
_____
_____
_____
_____
_____
_____
_____
_____

CONTINUITY SYNOPSIS/ONE LINE

TITLE:_____   PROD. NO._____

DIRECTOR:_____   DATE:._____

SCENE NOS.	SET	DESCRIPTION	D/N	PAGES	CHARACTERS

WARDROBE OUTLINE

TITLE _____   Time Breakdown_____

Scene Nos.   Sets   Date Shot
_____   _____   _____
_____   _____   _____
_____   _____   _____
_____   _____   _____
_____   _____   _____
_____   _____   _____
_____   _____   _____
_____   _____   _____

CHARACTERS

_____   _____

_____   _____
_____   _____

_____   _____
_____   _____

_____   _____
_____   _____

_____   _____

Index

217